BYZANTINE
CHRISTIANITY

BYZANTINE CHRISTIANITY

A very brief history

AVERIL CAMERON

First published in Great Britain in 2017

Society for Promoting Christian Knowledge
36 Causton Street
London SW1P 4ST
www.spck.org.uk

British Library Cataloguing-in-Publication Data
A catalogue record for this book is available from the British Library

ISBN 978–0–281–07613–0
eBook ISBN 978–0–281–07614–7

Typeset by Manila Typesetting Company
First printed in Great Britain by Ashford Colour Press
Subsequently digitally printed in Great Britain

eBook by Manila Typesetting Company

Produced on paper from sustainable forests

For my grandson, Silas Alexander,
who arrived in the world as I was finishing this book

Contents

Preface

A very short book about Byzantine Christianity represents a tall order, but I must nevertheless thank SPCK for the invitation to attempt it. The brief was to divide the text into two parts, covering history and legacy respectively. The history of Byzantine Christianity is relatively straightforward, but only relatively – some of the subject matter is very complicated, though I have tried to make it as accessible as possible. Many readers might also feel that the ordinary person and his or her religiosity get rather short shrift here, and I wish there could have been more on that. Tracing the legacy of Byzantine Christianity is more complex than it may at first seem. In one sense it has left a clear legacy to Orthodox countries and churches today, though the latter are many, and attempting to describe them briefly is extremely difficult. But its influence and importance go far deeper than this suggests, and deeper than many readers may suspect. Byzantine Christianity – that is, the forms of Christianity (the plural is intentional) found in the eastern Mediterranean region that was home to the very beginnings of the Christian faith – took shape in an undivided Christian world. When the Emperor Constantine founded Constantinople in AD 330, marking on most views the beginning of the Byzantine empire, he found that Christians disagreed among themselves, but the Church was still undivided. Byzantine Christianity developed its own characteristics, but it also belongs directly to the history of early Christianity; it should not be seen as something different and strange. The divide between eastern and western Christianity came only much later and more slowly and gradually than is often thought.

The aim of this book is to make Byzantine Christianity and its legacy better understood. Any such attempt will inevitably be highly personal and selective. But at a time when the connection between religion and politics is so much to the fore and of such critical importance, it is more essential than ever to appreciate the history of eastern Christianity as well as that of the west.

I am very grateful to Philip Law of SPCK, whose invitation to write this book was given during a conversation at the 17th International Conference of Patristic Studies in Oxford in August 2015. These conferences have been an important part of my life and I owe a great deal to the literally hundreds of colleagues and friends whom I have met and heard in the Examinations Schools at Oxford over many years. Many other colleagues have influenced the views expressed in this book, though they may well not agree with them, and I have profited from many conversations with James Pettifer about aspects of modern Orthodoxy. Finally I would like to thank the editorial staff at SPCK for making the publication process both speedy and relatively painless. I have often had occasion to realize that Byzantine Christianity is poorly understood except by specialists, and I hope that this book will help to fill what I feel is a real gap.

Averil Cameron
Keble College Oxford

Chronology

Chronology

Chronology

1397–1402	Constantinople besieged by the Ottoman Bayezid I
1402	Bayezid I defeated by the Mongol Tamurlane, Ankara
1430	Ottomans take Thessalonike
1438–9	Council of Ferrara/Florence
1444	Hungarians and western Crusaders defeated by Ottomans at Varna
1453	Fall of Constantinople to the Ottomans under Mehmet II

Part 1

THE HISTORY

1

What was Byzantium?

Byzantium and the Byzantine empire are usually associated with Eastern Orthodoxy. However, we need to start by clarifying both these concepts.

Byzantium

'Byzantium' and 'the Byzantine empire' generally refer to the empire ruled from Constantinople (modern Istanbul) and lasting from the dedication of the city by the Emperor Constantine in AD 330 until its fall to the Ottoman Turks in 1453. But there are some problems here. First, the term 'Byzantium' is modern and was not used by the Byzantines themselves (they called themselves Romans). Second, Constantinople was captured by the Fourth Crusade in 1204 and came under Latin rule until 1261, when the exiled Byzantines regained the city and re-established themselves there. Third, although Byzantium was indeed an empire for most of its history and ruled extensive territory, its size varied greatly at different periods. From its height after the wars of the Emperor Justinian in the sixth century, it lost much of its territory in the east as a result of the Arab conquests but recovered and grew again in the tenth to twelfth centuries. After the capture of Constantinople by the Fourth Crusade in 1204, it was reduced to several small enclaves or statelets ruled by various members and branches of the imperial family. The Byzantines from Nicaea recovered the city in 1261 but the territory ruled from Constantinople in its final phase was tiny compared with the empire's former glory.

For 150 years after its foundation, Constantinople was the seat of government of the eastern part of the Roman empire, and there were also Roman emperors ruling in the west. But the language of culture and administration in the east was Greek rather than Latin, and the gradual divergence of the eastern and western churches soon became apparent.

This book will leave these caveats aside and understand Byzantium and Byzantine as referring to the whole long period from the fourth to the fifteenth centuries.

A united Church

The early history of Byzantine Christianity is part of the history of Christianity itself. The first Christian communities developed in the eastern part of the Roman empire, and at the time of the Emperor Constantine (d. 337) there were still far more Christians there than in the west. The Church was still undivided, and would remain so for a long time yet. Byzantine Christianity was not something separate from early Christianity as a whole, and Christians today owe to it a great deal of what counts as Christian.

Orthodoxy

This is a book about Christianity in Byzantium, not about Orthodoxy, which is a narrower concept. In the Byzantine period the term 'orthodoxy' (lower case) embraced many differing beliefs and practices, and it is anachronistic simply to apply the term 'Orthodoxy' to Byzantium in the sense in which it refers to Eastern Orthodoxy today. The debt of the latter to Byzantine Christianity will be considered in Part 2.

There were many Christian groups both within and outside the Byzantine empire who passionately disagreed with each other, but all of whom considered themselves to be orthodox (meaning that they had the correct doctrine). The history of early Christianity is in part a story of struggles to assert one or another form of orthodox belief and practice. When Constantine decided to support the Christians he soon found, to his surprise and chagrin, that they did not all hold the same views. There had already been church councils or synods, but in a critically important move the emperor now called his own councils to attempt to settle matters. The Council of Nicaea (modern Iznik in western Turkey), summoned by Constantine in AD 325, was the first 'ecumenical' council; that is, it claimed to be a meeting of bishops from all over the Roman empire. In practice bishops from the western half of the empire were poorly represented, and the council was very far from the last word, even though it produced the first version of what became known as the Nicene Creed, still recited in eastern and western churches to this day. In later centuries the western habit of adding 'and from the Son' when referring to the Holy Spirit – known from the Latin as the *Filioque* – was to become one of the main sticking points between Rome and Constantinople, but the Creed of Nicaea, modified in 381, remained and remains common to both east and west. Six more councils were later also held to be ecumenical, the last in 787, again in Nicaea.

Within the Byzantine empire itself, continuing disagreements and increasing bad feeling in the later fifth and sixth centuries led to the formation of separatist churches in the eastern provinces (see Chapter 4), and after the Arab conquests of the 630s and 640s, many Christians lived under Islam; most spoke and wrote in languages other than Greek, though Greek also continued, and some, including the patriarchate of Jerusalem, stayed loyal to the teaching of the Council of Chalcedon (AD 451). When Constantinople seemed to be departing from it in the seventh century a major crisis ensued, involving bishops, monks and communities from the east all the way to Rome. It is important to remember that all sides involved in these painful divisions saw themselves as orthodox and the others as mistaken.

Again, while it is correct to say that today's Eastern Orthodox churches derive ultimately from Byzantium (see Chapter 11), and in some cases received their Christianity from Byzantine missions, we need to be cautious about applying the term 'Orthodoxy' to Byzantium itself.

Finally, Byzantine orthodoxy should not be straightforwardly identified with 'Greek Orthodoxy'. Despite the pre-eminence of the Greek language throughout the history of Byzantium, Greeks in an ethnic sense constituted only a tiny proportion of the population of an empire that stretched at its height from Italy to the borders of Iran, and included Egypt and a substantial part of North Africa. Indeed, Byzantine rule from Constantinople had to be reasserted in mainland Greece after an uncertain period following the arrival of the Slavs in the late sixth and early seventh centuries. Byzantium was conscious of its Hellenic heritage, preserved in language, culture and literature, but the Byzantine empire contained many different ethnic groups and many kinds of Christianity.

The Emperor Constantine (AD 306–37)

Constantine became sole emperor of the Roman world in 324 when he defeated his final rival, Licinius. It had taken him nearly 20 years to reach this position, from his father Constantius's death in York in 306, when Constantine was proclaimed emperor by Constantius's soldiers. In the years that followed, Constantine had gradually outmanoeuvred and eliminated other rivals until only his former ally Licinius remained. Constantine, his father Constantius and Licinius were all members of the ruling group known as the 'tetrarchy', set up by Diocletian in 293 in the hope of bringing stability to the empire after decades of crisis, and Constantine was no less ambitious and ruthless than the other members of the group. His final victory destroyed the tetrarchic model of power sharing; nevertheless, his decision to found and name his own new city on the site of Byzantion, an urban settlement going back to classical times, followed the tradition of other 'tetrarchic capitals', including that of Galerius in what is now Thessaloniki.

It is hard to know what Constantine's own religious beliefs really amounted to. He was said to have had a vision of the god Apollo while in Gaul in 310. Later, while on the way south through Italy to confront his rival Maxentius, he had a religious experience that seems to have impressed him enough to order the chi-rho (the first letters of the word 'Christ' in Greek) to be painted on his soldiers' shields. Eusebius, Bishop of Caesarea in Palestine, later claimed that the emperor had a vision of the cross in the sky with the words 'In this conquer'. Whatever the truth of these accounts, Constantine defeated Maxentius at the Milvian Bridge over the River Tiber in Rome late in 312, and immediately began to involve himself in Christian affairs. At the time Christians were only a tiny minority among his subjects and had until very recently been persecuted by his rivals. Licinius returned to the policy of persecution – at least in the version told by Constantine's propagandists – when he and Constantine went to war against each other some years later, but Constantine did not deviate from his determination to support Christianity.

From 324 to his death in 337, Constantine was the sole ruler of the Roman world. It is not clear, however, that Constantinople ('the city of Constantine') was intended by him to be a new capital to replace Rome. The seniority of Rome as an apostolic see continued to be accepted, and it took some time for Constantinople to become established as a leading Christian centre. In comparison with the number of churches he built in and around Rome, or the building of those he sponsored in and around Jerusalem, especially the Holy Sepulchre in Jerusalem and the Church of the Nativity in Bethlehem, in Constantinople Constantine seems to have been mainly interested in creating an imperial centre worthy of his new position, with an imperial palace, a hippodrome for chariot races, a splendid imperial way for processions and a statue of himself on a great column. He built an impressive imperial mausoleum with a controversial plan for his own burial, but the 'Great Church' of Hagia Sophia, or Saint Sophia ('Holy Wisdom'), was completed only by his son.

However, Constantine had a loyal publicist in Eusebius, Bishop of Caesarea, and the latter formulated a political philosophy according to which the emperor was God's vice-gerent on earth and the empire a microcosm of heaven. This was to have much mileage in later centuries.

By the end of the fourth century, Constantinople was a city with many churches and monasteries, whose bishop, or patriarch, was recognized as second only to that of Rome. Constantine did not and could not make Christianity the official religion of the empire, but the Emperor Julian, who tried to reverse the process but reigned only from 361 to 363, was the only emperor after Constantine who was not a Christian.

Constantine deferred to bishops and gave them a role in the justice system. He also made Sunday a day of rest; and even if this was not his intention, his repeal of Roman marriage legislation helped to open the way for Christians to choose celibacy and the ascetic life. Rulings made with his then ally, Licinius, in 313 gave the Church the legal standing it had not previously enjoyed, and while promising freedom of worship, made clear Constantine's preference for Christianity. The Church could now legally inherit wealth and property, an important change whose effect soon became apparent as rich people began to bequeath and donate their wealth to it. Constantine also delivered a remarkable address in which he suggested that the birth of Christ was the event prefigured in Virgil's Fourth Eclogue. By the time Constantine died, however, he had been influenced by those who had opposed the decisions at the Council of Nicaea and he was baptized by one of them.

After Constantine

Divisions continued after Constantine's death and throughout the fourth century, and were succeeded by others. But he had set the religion of the Roman empire on a new path. After him there was again often more than one emperor ruling at a time, and seats of government in both east and west. Milan and Ravenna, rather than Rome, were the homes of the imperial court in the west, but Rome retained its Christian prestige as the city of Saints Peter and Paul, and enjoyed recognized ecclesiastical primacy. From the last decade of the fourth century the east–west split was more pronounced, and in 476 the last Roman emperor in the west was deposed. The Emperor Justinian, ruling in Constantinople in the sixth century, fought lengthy wars to regain Roman control in the west, but with only limited success. By then Constantinople had been the seat of Christian emperors for 200 years and had grown to be a city of approaching half a million inhabitants. When the first church of Hagia Sophia was severely damaged by rioting and fire early in Justinian's reign, it was replaced with the great domed church that still stands. The dome was rebuilt later in the reign after earthquake damage, and centuries later became the model for the great mosques built in the city under Ottoman rule that dominate the sky-line of Istanbul today.

2

Monks, monasteries and bishops

This chapter and the next take as their starting point the formative period in Byzantine Christianity in the two centuries that followed the dedication of Constantinople in AD 330, when its main features took shape. The Church was already organized into bishoprics, and bishops were the leaders of their local congregations. Before Constantine, churches were relatively modest, but his example as a church builder and his enabling legislation opened the possibility of giving them new visibility in urban settings, a process assisted by the wealth that now found its way into the Church, as noted in Chapter 1. This wealth was in the control of bishops and was used not only for assisting the poor and needy but also for church building and associated needs.

Monks and ascetics

Christian advocacy of celibacy and sexual renunciation rather than marriage was already under way in the reign of Constantine. Individual men and women, especially in Egypt and Syria, began to live ascetic lives, sometimes retreating from cities to live in caves or in the desert, and the first half of the fourth century also saw the beginnings of organized monasticism. In Egypt, Pachomius was the founder of the first cenobitic monastery at Tabennisi, and this marked the start of the monastic movement that

11

became such a feature of Byzantine Christianity and the western Middle Ages. Byzantine monasticism was not centrally organized. Monasteries often began in informal ways, and groups of ascetics also lived together without being organized into a monastic complex with fixed rules. In the early fifth century, Palladius described male and female ascetics who pursued lives of chastity and renunciation in domestic settings in Constantinople. In some kinds of monasticism the monks would meet only for weekly communal worship; this is the model of the *lavra*, and it persisted in Byzantium alongside monasteries whose monks lived cenobitic or communal lives. Revered ascetic figures often attracted disciples who came to live near them. Before Pachomius, Saint Antony had already retreated into the desert in Egypt to lead an ascetic life, and when the great theologian Athanasius, Bishop of Alexandria, was forced into exile, he took refuge with monks in the desert. Athanasius's *Life of Antony*, composed soon after the saint's death in 356, is the first example of hagiography, or 'saints' lives', and was enormously influential in spreading the idea and ideals of asceticism.

It used to be thought that Egyptian monasticism was the inspiration for the rise of asceticism in Syria but it seems more likely that both developed over the same period. Syrian asceticism sometimes took exotic and individualistic forms, as we read in the account of it by the fifth-century bishop and theologian Theodoret of Cyrrhus (in northern Syria). Stylites, from the Greek word for 'pillar', like Symeon the Elder, who is said to have lived for 40 years on the top of a pillar at Qalat Siman in Syria, were also a feature of Syrian Christianity, though not confined to it (in the fifth century, Daniel the Stylite is said to have lived on a pillar near Constantinople for 33 years). Saint Basil, Bishop of Caesarea in Cappadocia, was the author of a rule for ceno-bitic monasteries that was widely followed later, while his sister, Macrina, lived in a less formal ascetic community based on her own household in the Pontus in what is now northern Turkey. Byzantine monasticism remained more varied than that in the west, and Basil's rule did not give rise to an order like that of Saint Benedict; the founders of later Byzantine monasteries often drew up or commis-sioned their own rules.

From their beginnings in the fourth century, monasteries became a major feature of Byzantine life, and in the fifth and sixth centuries monks also sometimes played an import-ant role in wider ecclesiastical affairs and were prominent in several turbulent episodes in fifth- and sixth-century Constantinople and other cities. Several large monasteries in Palestine were influential centres of ecclesiastical polit-ics in the sixth and seventh centuries. In the ninth century, monks of the Studios monastery in Constantinople were prominent in the opposition to the official iconoclastic pol-icy (see Chapter 5), and their abbot, Theodore the Studite, was imprisoned for it. The Studite monastery was also influential in the flowering of monastic culture and spir-ituality that followed the ending of the iconoclastic contro-versy. Elsewhere, different kinds of asceticism were practised together, as in the Judaean desert outside Jerusalem, where the remains of dozens of small and large monasteries and monastic cells are still visible. Few early monasteries are still functioning today, but Saint Catherine's, at the foot of Mount Sinai in Egypt, founded by Justinian in the mid sixth century, has had an unbroken monastic history until the present day. Finally, the role of monasteries illustrates very well the typically Byzantine mix of the public and formal and the intimate and private. We often hear in saints' lives of humble parents giving their child to live in a monastery from an early age to be brought up as a prospective monk. Many of those who entered monasteries – often called the 'angelic life' by contemporaries – were illiterate, and learned their letters and their theology, and sometimes also how to copy manuscripts, in the monastery.

Church building

The fourth to sixth centuries were also a period when many churches were built and when the typical Byzantine church decoration familiar from later periods had its beginning. Many early churches were built on the model of a Roman basilica, with side aisles and an apse, which might be decorated with mosaic; but some domed churches were also built, and these became much more common later. Depictions of the Virgin (Greek *Theotokos*, 'Bearer of God') in the apse begin to be found by the end of the sixth century. Liturgical needs also affected the layout of churches and their ancillary buildings. In many cases in the eastern empire, only the foundations of these early churches survive, but the walls of the church of the so-called Red Monastery in Egypt, recently restored, are covered with a striking range of frescoes of saints and scriptural scenes. The nearby White Monastery, whose decoration has not survived in the same way, was associated with a huge monastic complex led by the fifth-century abbot Shenoute.

Liturgical development went along with church building. The Spanish pilgrim Egeria travelled to Jerusalem in the late fourth century and left a detailed account in Latin of the liturgy she experienced there. The set of catechetical homilies composed by Cyril, Bishop of Jerusalem, in the mid fourth century gives a vivid impression of how candidates were prepared for the great ceremony of (adult) baptism, which involved extensive preparation, culminating in a great communal liturgy at Easter.

Bishops and their roles

Bishops now became members of an elite. Constantine turned to them for advice, claiming that important decisions on religious matters should be theirs. As well as judicial privileges, he provided them with travel to councils at state expense, and clergy were also exempted from taxes. But at the same time he set a precedent as emperor by taking an active role himself, and this ambiguity in the relation between the emperor and the Church persisted throughout the history of Byzantium.

The letters of Theodoret of Cyrrhus provide a window into the work and connections of a bishop in northern Syria in the fifth century. Besides his liturgical role in his cathedral church he was the leader of the local clergy and dealt with many local problems. He was also a controversial participant in wider church affairs, and a prolific author. Bishops also managed the resources of their diocese, which could be substantial. The extent of the requirement to give alms was much debated, especially as it applied to the rich, but it was also often bishops who built churches and other ecclesiastical buildings. Sometimes the two went together: Basil, for example, built an elaborate complex where the poor could be housed and their diseases treated. Some bishops became powerful players in doctrinal disputes. But above all, bishops were expected to preach and teach, and hundreds of examples survive of the homilies they delivered to their congregations. Bishops gradually became the leaders of urban society, rivals of the secular authorities in prestige. They often took the lead in public affairs, even in conditions of warfare such as the conflicts between Byzantium and Sasanian Iran in the sixth century.

By now, although Christianity was still by no means universal, the Church had become deeply embedded in Byzantine life. The passage from secular to monastic or ecclesiastical could be easy, and in later centuries even patriarchs of Constantinople had sometimes had lay careers, while many wealthy laypersons entered or founded monasteries in later life. Finally, the monasteries fostered a rich tradition of spirituality that still shapes eastern Christianity today (see Part 2).

Parallel structures? The 'harmony' between Church and state

Many Byzantine emperors acted in a high-handed manner in relation to church affairs, but as we have seen, they were not heads of the Church, as is implied by the term 'Caesaropapism' (often encountered in older books), and did not always get their way. In Constantinople a standing synod of bishops led by the bishop or patriarch could rule on a variety of ecclesiastical issues, and was sometimes strongly opposed to emperors, for example when in the seventh century Heraclius married his niece, or when in the tenth century the Emperor Leo VI married for the fourth time against church rules. Some patriarchs of Constantinople were deposed by emperors, but equally, some emperors also fell foul of powerful patriarchs. In theory, Church and state existed in harmony together, but this did not prevent frequent tension. Perhaps as a result of this ambiguity the Byzantine Church did not develop into a powerful independent institution like the Roman papacy, and in contrast with western Europe the closeness of emperor and Church was not affected by new political formations. These issues, and the relation between Church and state in some contemporary Orthodox countries, are discussed later (see Chapters 14 and 15).

3

The age of the Fathers

Byzantine Christianity was deeply influenced by the teachings of the Greek Fathers. Go into any Byzantine church building and you will see them depicted in mosaic or fresco, wearing distinctive black and white robes. The 'three hierarchs', the fourth-century bishops Basil, Gregory of Nazianzus and John Chrysostom, are venerated today as the founding Fathers of Orthodoxy (Basil, Gregory and Basil's brother Gregory of Nyssa, also a fourth-century bishop, are also often known as the 'Cappadocians', after the location of their sees in modern Turkey). We call the age of the Fathers the 'patristic period', after the Latin word for 'Fathers' (the 'Desert Mothers' some people talk about tend to be individual female ascetics rather than the writers and authorities, or indeed bishops, discussed here). Some limit the term 'patristic' to a shorter chronological span, but many would agree that the last, and one of the greatest, patristic authorities was the eighth-century theologian John of Damascus, who spent his life under Islamic rule. It has been supposed that John wrote his many works as a monk in the monastery of Saint Sabas not far from Bethlehem (a monastery still functioning today), but he was more probably based in Jerusalem. Another great Byzantine theologian, also a monastic writer, was the seventh-century Maximus the Confessor, who came from one of the major Palestinian monasteries and travelled across the Mediterranean to Rome, with a period in a monastic community in Byzantine North Africa. Maximus played a leading role in the resistance to imperial religious policy and was heavily involved in a synod in Rome in 649 that condemned it; for this he was mutilated and died in exile in Thrace in 662. He too was the author of numerous theological works in Greek that became immensely influential in Byzantium and are still so today.

The golden age and its legacy

The fourth and early fifth centuries are often regarded as the golden age of Greek patristic literature. Many of the prominent bishops of this period were also prolific authors, the founders of a Christian literature in Greek that was influential throughout Byzantine history and remains so today. The writings of Athanasius, Bishop of Alexandria, are still basic for the understanding of Trinitarian theology, and we shall meet Cyril, one of his successors, again later in this chapter. Basil, Gregory of Nazianzus and Gregory of Nyssa all wrote treatises, homilies and expositions of Scripture that were continually cited and used by later generations. John Chrysostom, Bishop of Constantinople at the end of the fourth century, was an amazingly prolific writer, whose homilies not only expounded Scripture but also laid out the moral behaviour expected of his well-to-do congregation. As a priest in Antioch he had been a prominent speaker in urban and imperial politics, and now he was not afraid to castigate the liking of the rich ladies in his congregation for make-up, jewellery and elaborate dress, or even to criticize the empress publicly.

These men had been educated in the traditional classical way; they achieved prominent positions and used their education to promote Christianity in a world in which Christianity was still far from dominant. They belonged to well-established networks and exchanged hundreds of letters. Their theological and pastoral writing set a pattern that was followed by many others throughout the later centuries of Byzantium. Their works were read and they were cited as authorities – and their opinions sometimes argued over – in innumerable later contexts.

Not all the Fathers were bishops, nor did they all write in Greek. The so-called 'Desert Fathers' of Egypt were monks in the desert monasteries who have left large numbers of 'Sayings', which were highly influential on later Byzantine monasticism. In the fourth century, Evagrius Ponticus, a controversial but important writer on Christian spirituality, was a monk in Constantinople who went to Egypt and spent the rest of his life there. Further east, Ephrem the Syrian was a monk who wrote hymns, commentaries and many other works in Syriac in Nisibis (Nusaybin, on the modern Turkish border with Syria), and Edessa in Mesopotamia (now Sanliurfa in eastern Turkey). A little later, Shenoute, the abbot of the White Monastery (see Chapter 2), a double monastery for men and women at Sohag in Egypt, produced a vast amount of writings in Coptic that are only now beginning to be edited and translated. A large number of other patristic writers can be added to the list, and the overall volume of their writings is enormous.

Some important ascetic writings belong to this period, and it was now that the fundamentals of Byzantine spirituality evolved. The Desert Fathers, and the writings of ascetics such as Evagrius, Macarius and Diadochus, established a pattern of spiritual guidance that became central for Byzantine Christians and for later Orthodox Christians.

Their writings were copied, read and collected into syntheses and compilations over many centuries. Important conceptions in Byzantine Christianity such as contrition and repentance, as well as inwardness and the centrality of quietness and prayer, all took shape in this period. More than any other, it was the patristic period and the age of asceticism that gave Byzantine Christianity its key characteristics.

Theological divisions

Defending and explaining Christian orthodoxy and attacking heresy were central issues, and these deep disagreements were also felt among the desert monks and ascetics. The Council of Nicaea in 325 exiled the Egyptian priest Arius for arguing that the Father and the Son were not consubstantial, but 'Arianism', or differing versions of it, remained a lively issue throughout the fourth century, and many other variant teachings were also targeted in patristic writing. Doctrinal divisions of different kinds persisted for centuries. These arguments about doctrine mattered greatly, even if many people could not follow the finer points. Even in the last period of Byzantium, Byzantines were still arguing about the meaning of key scriptural and other texts.

Byzantium had inherited the condemnation of 'heresy' from early Christianity, but now heretics were formally condemned – anathematized (in fact cursed), exiled and deposed (if they were bishops) – and were the targets of a vast body of polemical writing. With the ending of iconoclastic policies in 843, an official document known as the 'Synodicon of Orthodoxy' condemned the wrong beliefs and practices that had been officially proscribed. It was brought up to date in later periods with the addition of more names, and read out in churches on the first Sunday of Lent. Similarly strong language was continually used by bishops and others (and by the 'heretics' themselves), and was also addressed to Jews and later to Muslims. Converts from Judaism or Islam were required to sign statements abjuring and condemning their former beliefs. How far this language of abuse and the actual practice of enforcing orthodoxy demonstrate an overall intolerance is a difficult question, and the notion of 'economy' (see Chapter 13) was not infrequently invoked to justify a departure from what might normally be expected, or as we would now say, a bending of the rules. Nevertheless bishops, even including the patriarch of Constantinople, were not infrequently deposed and exiled, and the condemnatory language that was frequently used was not just a matter of empty threats.

Councils

The Council of Nicaea was called in the hope of settling divergent beliefs and practices within the Church (including getting agreement on the date of Easter). This was the first ecumenical (literally 'of the world'; that is, of the whole Church) council, as opposed to local ones, usually known as 'synods'. As we have seen, it was not the last: six more councils counted as ecumenical and relating to the western as well as the eastern Church were held at Constantinople (381), Ephesus (431), Chalcedon (451), Constantinople (553, 680–1) and Nicaea (787). All were called to settle controversies, but most in turn gave rise to further division, or even to splits in the Church. Nevertheless they were regarded as fundamental and are depicted in Byzantine art as marking the constituents of correct belief. They issued acts (records of the meetings), not all of which have survived (for instance, the acts of the council of 553 survive only in Latin translation); those present were required to sign the official record. Some, but not all, also issued canons, sets of ecclesiastical rulings; the so-called Quinisext Council of 692 was called in order to draw up such canons because neither of the last two councils had done so. The Council of Ephesus in 431 was followed by a second council in 449, which was not accepted later as ecumenical and which led quickly to the summoning of the Council of Chalcedon, at which its conclusions were repudiated. The Lateran Synod of 649 held in Rome to oppose the then official Byzantine doctrine of Monothelitism (the belief that Christ had one will rather than two, a human and a divine), was not an ecumenical council. Thirty years later, the Sixth Council, held in Constantinople (680–1), condemned Monothelitism and reversed imperial policy. The Second Council of Nicaea in 787 condemned the previously official position of opposition to religious images, stated at a council at Hieria, near Constantinople, in 754, but was itself followed by a further iconoclast council before the controversy finally ended in 843 (see Chapter 5). All the ecumenical councils were regarded as applying in the west as well as the east, but as the eastern and western churches drew apart, the council of 787 was the last ecumenical council in this sense.

It was the Council of Constantinople in 381 that confirmed what we now know as the Nicene Creed, and the Council of Ephesus in 431 that endorsed the title of *Theotokos*, 'Bearer of God', for the Virgin Mary, and condemned Nestorius, Bishop of Constantinople, for opposing it. This led eventually to the formation of a separatist church, often wrongly called 'Nestorian' but better termed the 'Church of the East', which became strong in Syria, the Sasanian empire and across eastern Eurasia, even reaching Xi'an in China in the 630s (see Chapter 4). The Council of Chalcedon in 451 was even more divisive. It aimed to settle the disputed question of how Christ could be both divine and human. The Church of the East emphasized a single, human, nature (Greek *phusis*) in Christ, but before and during the Council of Ephesus, Cyril of Alexandria had stressed Christ's divine nature, and he was followed by many others, including Severus, who became patriarch of Antioch in the early sixth century and was deposed by the Emperor Justin I in 518. The Council of Chalcedon affirmed the doctrine of two natures united in Christ, and its adherents are therefore sometimes called 'dyophysites'. In the context of the Second Council of Ephesus in 449 (see above), Pope Leo I issued a decree – the Tome of Leo, Greek *tomos* – that was much cited in the discussions around the Council of Chalcedon in 451.

In the case of the followers of Cyril and Severus, the opposition that followed did not result in an actual split until later in the sixth century, and the Fifth Council, held in Constantinople in 553, attempted to reconcile the differing positions (see Chapter 4). This was only one of several strenuous efforts towards reconciliation in the sixth century, combined however with periods of persecution. The seventh-century formulations of one energy or one will in Christ also attempted to resolve matters, but were both resisted by the pro-Chalcedonian dyophysites; the most prominent of these were Maximus Confessor and Pope Martin I, who like Maximus was arrested in Rome as a result and died in exile in 655.

4

The eastern Church splits

The Emperor Justinian (527–65) was one of the most formidable of Byzantine emperors and is well known from the mosaics of him and his wife, Theodora, in the church of San Vitale, Ravenna. Early in his reign, Justinian's troops were engaged in operations in the east against the Sasanians, and in 533 he launched a military expedition to expel the Vandals who had ruled Roman North Africa for a century. Justinian claimed to have had a prophetic dream, and the expedition under his general Belisarius was spectacularly successful, driving out the Vandals in a matter of months and establishing Byzantine rule. Justinian followed this with a similar expedition to Italy, which was ruled by the Ostrogoths, but that was another story, and the Gothic war dragged on until 554. Meanwhile there was renewed warfare on the eastern front and Byzantium had to pay a heavy price when peace was eventually made in 561. This did not prevent a further bitter war between Byzantium and Persia at the end of the century or a successful invasion by Persia in the early seventh. Jerusalem was captured by the Persians in 614.

Did Justinian hope to regain the whole of the western empire, lost to Rome since the late fifth century? If so, he failed, and his wars were a heavy drain on the empire's resources. But Justinian also codified Roman law in the *Codex Justinianus* and his lawyers drew up further legal compilations, the *Digest* and the *Institutes*, all in the years

528 to 534 (his later laws, being new, were known as *Novels*). In 532 he escaped a serious revolt that did much damage, and built the present church of Hagia Sophia in Constantinople on the site of the old one (see Chapter 1).

Justinian was keen to extend Christianity beyond the borders of the empire through political relations with states reaching from Ethiopia to the Caucasus, and he tried very hard to settle church affairs internally. He was a patron of new church building and restoration in North Africa and many other areas, building a grand new church of the Virgin in Jerusalem and founding the monastery of Saint Catherine (originally dedicated to the Transfiguration) at the foot of Mount Sinai. He was a keen theologian who composed doctrinal statements himself, and he struggled to reconcile opposing factions within the Church, resorting to theological initiatives of his own. However, Justinian's bullying of Pope Vigilius in the context of the Council of 553 proved counterproductive, while in the east, anti-Chalcedonian miaphysites, who held that Christ had only one divine nature, also often called monophysites, were already ordaining their own clergy. During the next decades their numbers in Palestine and Syria[1] increased, although the Greek-speaking monasteries of Palestine and the patriarchate of Jerusalem held to the Chalcedonian formula of two natures and later became known locally by the disparaging term 'Melkites', from the Syriac for 'king', as being on the side of the emperor. When Arab armies arrived in Syria in 634, the Christian population was split. Not only were there both dyophysites and miaphysites; still others held the view that Christ had only a human nature.

---

1 This term is used to denote a larger area than the modern state of Syria.

These splits and the communities that arose from them lie behind some of the complex divisions between Christians in the Middle East today. The region was also split linguistically. While the Chalcedonian monasteries and the Jerusalem patriarchate used Greek (though Saint Catherine's and Saint Sabas later became multilingual centres), miaphysitism was strong among Syriac-speakers, as was the Church of the East. Throughout this period of gradual separation, polemical works were written on all sides. The miaphysite Syriac-speaking church was called pejoratively 'Jacobite' by its opponents, after Jacob Bar'adai, one of its founders, but the fact that it is more properly called the 'Syrian Orthodox Church' is an indicator of the importance attached to the orthodox label.[2] The Syriac-speaking miaphysites built on a learned tradition dating from the age of Ephrem in the fourth century (see Chapter 3), and now monasteries such as Qenneshrin in northern Syria developed into impressive seats of learning comparable with the East Syrian school at Nisibis.

Christian literature in Syriac was not a new development. Christians had already been using this version of Aramaic for centuries, and a 'harmony' of the four Gospels in Syriac already existed in the second century. A huge volume of Christian writing in Syriac survives, especially from the fifth century onwards, and it continued long into the Islamic period. Greek works were translated into Syriac, and Syriac was an important vehicle through which Greek philosophy and science reached Baghdad and played a major role in the flowering of scholarship in Arabic in the ninth century. Christian writers in Syriac were also prominent in

---

2 Modern historians also call its members West Syrian, to distinguish them from the 'Nestorian' East Syrians.

engaging in theological dialogue with Islam after the Arab conquest and throughout the medieval period.

Even after the conquests, Greek was still used by Chalcedonian theologians, as we can see from the example of John of Damascus (see Chapter 3). Cosmas, one of the most important hymnographers, and said to have been the foster-brother of John of Damascus, belonged to the monastery of Saint Sabas in the eighth century and later became bishop of Gaza. There were also contacts with Constantinople. Two brothers, Theodore and Theophanes, known as the 'Grapti', went from the monastery of Saint Sabas to Constantinople in the early ninth century, where they were stalwart defenders of religious images and suffered periods of exile. Another monk of Saint Sabas was Michael Syncellus, who also went to Constantinople and suffered, like the Grapti, for his defence of images but survived to become the abbot of the Chora monastery in Constantinople (now well known as the much-visited Kariye Djami). Michael was the author of a treatise on syntax that was much read later, as well as hymns, hagiography and other works.

The Church in Egypt

A complex pattern can also be seen in Egypt in the period between the Councils of Ephesus and Chalcedon and the Arab conquest of Egypt in 641. Cyril of Alexandria, patriarch of Alexandria in the early fifth century, was a powerful and controversial bishop and theologian who placed a strong emphasis on the divinity of Christ. He was succeeded by others who were equally forceful during the various disputes of the fifth and early sixth centuries: Dioscorus, supporter of the miaphysite monk Eutyches, who presided over the Second Council of Ephesus in 449 but was deposed and exiled by the Council of Chalcedon two years later, and Timothy Aelurus, who became patriarch in 457 and was twice exiled for his miaphysite activity. Severus of Antioch also went to Egypt after he was deposed and exiled from Antioch in 512. The rivalry between Chalcedonians and miaphysites in Egypt continued into the seventh century, and allegiances were split. At the time of the Arab conquest the patriarch, Cyrus, was Chalcedonian but had a rival in the miaphysite Benjamin, who was driven into hiding but then returned. The miaphysites had the powerful advantage of seeing themselves as the victims of persecution, as shown in the miaphysite *Life* of Saint Samuel, a monk at Scetis. We remember now that Egypt was lost to the Byzantine empire with the Arab conquests, and the modern Coptic Orthodox Church is one of the non-Chalcedonian eastern churches, but this transition did not happen overnight.

As is also the case with the miaphysites in Syria, it is often said that the Copts hated Constantinople and welcomed or assisted the Arab invaders, but this is hard to demonstrate from the contemporary evidence. As is also true of 'Syriac', the term 'Coptic' does not indicate ethnicity but the name of a language (a form of Egyptian, written in an alphabet drawing heavily on Greek). It is derived from Arabic and despite common usage it should not be used with reference to this period to designate a people (the Christian population of Egypt, or the non-elite), a religion or a cultural style.

Other non-Chalcedonian churches

Christianity in Ethiopia is very ancient and was much influenced from the important patriarchate of Alexandria.

As a result of the divisions in the period we have been discussing, Ethiopian Christianity followed the lead of Egypt, and the present-day Ethiopian Orthodox Church is also non-Chalcedonian.

Georgia and Armenia also lay claim to very ancient Christian traditions. While the Georgians stayed in communion with Constantinople, the Armenians rejected the Chalcedonian formula at the Second Council of Dvin in 554, but they also rejected miaphysitism and adhered to the teaching of Cyril of Alexandria. However, there were also many Chalcedonians in Armenia, and Byzantium made efforts in the late sixth century to promote adherence to Chalcedon; this was continued by the Emperor Heraclius while on his Persian campaign in the 620s. Nevertheless in the eighth century union was declared with the Syrian Orthodox. In the tenth and eleventh centuries, Byzantium gained control of much of Armenia, but this came to an end with the Byzantine defeat at Manzikert in 1071, and until the fifteenth century the Armenian *catholicos*, or head of the Church, had his base in Cilicia in modern Turkey. Renewed attempts at union in the twelfth century failed on the death of the Emperor Manuel I Comnenus in 1180, and the Armenians turned to the Latins instead. There were also differences of practice with Byzantium, the Armenian Church sharing with the Latins the use of unleavened bread (*azymes*) as well as unmixed wine for the Eucharist.

Islam and the Arab conquests

The hard-fought war against Sasanian Persia in the 620s had only just ended, with the recovery of Jerusalem from

Persian occupation, when the Arabs attacked Syria and what have become known as the Arab conquests began. The fragments of the True Cross had been taken from Jerusalem to Ctesiphon, and the Emperor Heraclius returned the Cross to Jerusalem with solemn pomp in 630. But the Byzantine army was defeated in Battle at the River Yarmuk in 636 and Heraclius retreated; the strength was no longer there to fight another enemy and these incursions may in fact not have seemed a long-term threat. Heraclius turned his attention to doctrinal matters, inspiring strong opposition to his one-energy and one-will formulations (Chapter 3) but ensuring that the latter became official Byzantine policy for the next generation. But the Arabs were there to stay. Many towns surrendered, and by 640, Jerusalem was in Muslim hands. Egypt fell in 641 and Arab armies entered North Africa. Much of Anatolia was also lost. Byzantium's old enemy, the Sasanians, had collapsed but a new enemy had arisen.

The Arab conquests changed the size, shape and focus of the Byzantine empire. At first the numbers of Muslims in Umayyad Syria were small, but despite being recognized as a People of the Book, Christians were increasingly regarded as second-class citizens. Nevertheless Christians under Islam found ways of living and even prospering, and Christian culture continued. The many small monastic settlements in the Judaean desert fell into decline, but this was only gradual. Jews, the other People of the Book, were suspected by Christians of assisting both the Persian and the Arab invaders, and the level of hostility to Jews was very high. Under Muslim rule they found somewhat less prejudice, and Tiberias, for example, flourished as a major centre of Jewish scholarship.

Constantinople itself withstood Arab sieges, and some of the Byzantine military and naval campaigns against the Arabs met with success; but the loss of so much territory was a very serious blow and meant that huge numbers of Christians no longer belonged to the Byzantine empire.

5

Icons and iconoclasm

During the eighth and ninth centuries the Byzantine Church went through a period of intense controversy that in many ways defined its later characteristics, and in the longer term reinforced the shift away from the Roman Church. There were two phases in what is usually termed the 'iconoclastic controversy', or simply 'iconoclasm', shorthand for an opposition to religious images that received official support. The first phase began either in 726 or more likely 730, when the patriarch Germanus was deposed, and lasted until the Second Council of Nicaea in 787; the second ran from 787 to the ending of iconoclasm in 843. In the first phase, objections to religious images centred on charges of idolatry and the place of matter in the divine economy (see Chapter 13), whereas in the second, theological writers moved towards a philosophical debate about the relation of image and archetype. By the 840s, after changes in the major actors and the historical circumstances, together with many episcopal depositions, imprisonments and changes of position by individuals, the appetite for further struggle had worn itself out and religious images were officially restored under the Empress Theodora and her young son Michael III.

The restoration of images took place after a synod but without a further full council, and was followed by the issuing of the document known as the 'Synodicon of

Orthodoxy' (see Chapter 3) and celebrated as 'the Triumph of Orthodoxy' (it is depicted in stylized fashion in an early sixteenth-century icon of that name in the British Museum, showing Theodora, the young Michael III and church leaders standing round an icon of the Mother of God). It was marked by a new liturgical Feast of Orthodoxy during which the Synodicon or parts of it were read. With its later additions, the Synodicon became a fundamental document for the Byzantine Church, and its teaching on images was reaffirmed after a further – though comparatively minor – dispute about images in the early twelfth century.

Religious images, portrayals of Christ, the Virgin and the saints, could come in different forms (the Greek word *eikon* simply means likeness), from mosaics and frescoes in churches to ivory reliefs. But the word 'icon' is mainly associated with the portable images, usually on wood, now familiar from Orthodox churches and from countless reproductions. For many people they are what most obviously distinguishes an Orthodox church and Orthodox practice from the western tradition. Bowing down in front of icons, as Orthodox worshippers do, was defended by John of Damascus as veneration rather than worship; he argued that it does not constitute idolatry because the veneration goes to the person depicted, not the image itself.

Few icons have survived from before the iconoclast period, except in Rome and at Saint Catherine's monastery on Sinai, neither of which was reached by iconoclasm. However, written evidence suggests that their popularity had been increasing, and stories already circulated about their miraculous properties. This development seems to have been spontaneous and unregulated, and it revived anxieties previously voiced about the propriety of Christian images.

A great deal remains unclear about the main events during the controversy and the actual extent of the iconoclast threat. This is partly because historians disagree, but more importantly because we have to rely on iconophile (pro-image) sources that are later and very one-sided. There was clearly a later purge of iconoclast writing by the successful iconophiles (though indeed the iconoclasts themselves also did their best to find and burn iconophile books). Among iconoclastic texts, the *Enquiries*, attributed to the iconoclast Emperor Constantine V (741–75), only survives in fragments, and the acts of the iconoclast council held at Hieria in 754 can only be reconstructed indirectly. Whether iconoclasm was a reform movement within Byzantine Christianity in reaction to the successes of the Arabs and Islam (Constantinople had endured a dangerous Arab siege in 717), and to recent natural disasters, or an internal response to the growing prominence of images and an assertion of imperial authority against centrifugal tendencies within the Church remains uncertain; probably all these factors were in play. Some historians play down the involvement of the Emperor Leo III (717–41), but his son Constantine V involved himself in iconoclastic policies directly and was vilified for it by iconophile writers. Constantine was also opposed to relics and the cult of the saints, and subjected monks to humiliating punishments; the only true image was held to be the Eucharist. The Empress Irene – 'a mere woman', in the words of a ninth-century writer – reigned as regent for her son at the time of the iconophile Council of 787, but her deposition from the throne in 802 opened the way to a renewal of iconoclasm before icons were finally restored. The controversy thus extended over many decades, and these were turbulent times in which churchmen in the capital were obliged to make their allegiance public. Some clearly changed sides.

The actual extent of iconoclastic damage, and of iconoclast persecution, is somewhat unclear. Both seem to have been limited. We hear of some high-profile examples of the white-washing or plastering over of images in churches, including Hagia Sophia in Constantinople, where the later restoration of the mosaic of the Virgin in the apse was celebrated in a homily by the patriarch Photius in AD 867 (see Chapter 6, and the cover illustration to this book). Constantine V is credited with having replaced images of the six ecumenical councils in Constantinople with a depiction of charioteers, and with destroying images of Christ at the church of Blachernae, and there is some evidence of the covering up of images or replacement by plain crosses elsewhere. But it would be wrong to imagine an empire-wide campaign of destruction. As for persecution, the *Life* of Saint Stephen the Younger extols Stephen as a martyr in the cause of images during the reign of Constantine V, and many other heroic tales of resistance were told, some of them relating to women. However, men and women alike defended images and resisted pressure. Theodore, abbot of the Studite monastery in Constantinople, was exiled and imprisoned after opposing an iconoclast council in 815. During his imprisonment he was beaten and moved from one place to another but was still able to write hundreds of letters in favour of images, to both lay and ecclesiastical contacts. Theodore had also been exiled before after leading the opposition against the elevation of Nicephorus, a layman, as patriarch in 806, and Nicephorus himself was exiled for opposing the iconoclast council of 815.

The argument from tradition was very important, and defenders of religious images had to find a way of reconciling their views with the clear prohibition of graven images in the Second Commandment. Appeal was therefore made to an 'unwritten' tradition, and collections made of passages from the Fathers that might seem to support images. Such was the level of effort involved that strict measures were taken at the Council of 787 to prevent the falsification of citations, following a precedent already set. The argument about images was also focused on the representation of the divine, for which pictures were claimed to be superior to words. It can further be seen as christological, since it asked the question of whether the divine nature of Christ could be depicted, or only the human, and whether depicting Christ circumscribed his divinity.

The final restoration of images after so long a period of controversy made possible a new freedom and energy in Byzantine monasticism, and it was followed by the unhindered development of new schemes of church decoration based on the narrative and symbolic use of religious images. This coincided with a revival of learning that was already underway, and with the copying of manuscripts in minuscule script rather than the earlier and more cumbersome uncial. The iconoclast controversy did not dominate the whole period, but in many ways the restoration of images shaped the Byzantine Church for the centuries to come. It was also a triumph of tradition over reform. More upheavals were to come in later centuries, but this challenge had been defeated.

Key figures: John of Damascus and Nicephorus

We have already met John of Damascus as a theologian and monk writing in Greek under the Umayyad caliphate, most probably in Jerusalem; according to tradition, his family and John himself had served the Muslim administration in Damascus. John was known in Constantinople as a defender of images and was attacked and condemned by the iconoclast Council of 754. His three treatises in defence of images, in fact three versions of his overall argument composed perhaps just before and just after 730 (the third may be later), address the charge of idolatry, defend the place of matter in the divine economy (see Chapter 13) and set out the difference between worship and veneration; John also attacks the right of emperors to make rules for the Church.

John deployed the argument from tradition in a way already familiar from earlier patristic literature, and each treatise is accompanied by a *florilegium*, or list of patristic citations, in defence of images. *Florilegia* were also deployed in the debates at the Second Council of Nicaea, and the circumstances of their compilation and the relation between the various examples are very complex. There were also local versions of iconoclasm, but John also seems to be writing entirely within the Greek patristic tradition. Further, his arguments drew on an existing tradition of Christian argumentation against Judaism. Puzzles remain about when and how his writings reached Constantinople and about the texts themselves, but their importance is high as an expression of the arguments against iconoclasm in its first phase.

Important works in defence of images in the second phase of iconoclasm were written by the patriarch Nicephorus (806–15), both before and after his stand against the council of 815 leading to his exile, and consist of an *Apology* and three treatises; he also attempted, unsuccessfully, to win over the Emperor Leo V and his successor Michael II.

Nicephorus's predecessor as patriarch, Tarasius (elevated as a layman like Nicephorus), had composed a refutation of the decree of the iconoclastic council of 754, and Nicephorus's own treatises are long and detailed, reflecting the way the argument had moved on since the time of John of Damascus. Nicephorus addresses the objection that the divine cannot be circumscribed, and the issue of the relation of the image to the archetype, and answers the arguments in Constantine V's *Enquiries*, but also ranges widely over earlier heresies and launches an attack on Constantine V, contrasting him with good emperors of the past and arguing that iconoclasm has damaged the empire.

These were not the only works by Nicephorus in which he attacked the arguments of the iconoclasts. The last was a refutation of the decree of the iconoclast council of 815 and an attack on the authenticity of the passages cited in its *florilegium*, which had drawn on citations drawn up for the iconoclast council of 754 – according to Nicephorus's biographer the latter were clearly falsified, as Nicephorus sought to argue. The same writer says that iconophile bishops were brought in chains before the council and humiliated.

Iconoclasm was an attack on the use of religious images, but it was also a war of words, and sometimes more than words. We hear most about events and arguments among the elite than ordinary people, and the iconophile sources must be regarded with suspicion; but references to icons in private homes indicate that the dispute did indeed reach more widely.

6

After iconoclasm

At the end of March 867, the patriarch Photius delivered a homily celebrating the mosaic of the Virgin now to be seen in the apse of Hagia Sophia in Constantinople, illustrated on the cover of this book. It was the first such decoration after the ending of iconoclasm, and Photius says that whereas until then the church had only 'shed but faint rays from its face to visitors', now the Virgin could be seen in a lifelike image. His triumphal tone vividly conveys the sense of liberation felt by the victorious iconophiles. Manuscript illustrations depicted the iconoclasts in the guise of Jews attacking images, and patronage of new decorative cycles was made possible without hindrance in churches and monasteries.

This was an age when powerful personalities clashed, and in so doing exposed growing fault lines between the western and Byzantine churches. One of them was the same Photius, the nephew of the patriarch Tarasius, and himself elevated from lay status to patriarch. He was a bureaucrat and a scholar, known for his *Bibliotheca*, a kind of handlist of the large number of books he had read, which included many classical works. His appointment in 858 caused a clash with another formidable character, Pope Nicholas I, who supported Photius's predecessor Ignatius and considered Photius's elevation uncanonical. Photius was exiled in 867, but restored in 877 when Ignatius died. He was on the wrong side again when the Emperor Basil I died in 886, as a supporter of Basil against the latter's son Leo, and when Leo became emperor as Leo VI, Photius was exiled a second time.

Photius was elevated when the papacy was growing in power and as the west and Constantinople were competing for influence in the Balkans. The dispute between Photius and Pope Nicholas marked an early stage in a long process leading to schism between Rome and Constantinople. In 867 Photius held a synod in Constantinople that excommunicated the pope and condemned western errors, including the addition of the words 'and from the Son' to the mention of the Holy Spirit in the Creed. This issue became known as the *Filioque*, Latin for 'and the Son'. But the murder of Michael III by his co-emperor Basil soon followed. Basil became sole emperor and was in no mood for a clash with Rome. Photius was deposed and it is claimed that the acts of his council were burnt.

Together with Rome's claim to primacy, the 'procession' of the Holy Spirit – that is, whether the Holy Spirit proceeded from the Father and the Son or only from the Father – became a central issue between the Roman and Byzantine churches throughout the rest of the Byzantine period. The addition in Latin of *Filioque* had not been formally adopted in Rome but was in use elsewhere in the west. After Photius it continued to be argued over in countless treatises and other works by later Byzantine writers, as well as in councils and works by Latins, with neither side managing to convince the other. It remains a difference between eastern and western Christianity to this day.

Byzantines and Slavs

In the summer of 860, after the Emperor Michael III had left to confront the Arabs in the east, a large fleet suddenly appeared in the Bosphorus and started attacking the suburbs of Constantinople. These invaders were the Rus', Scandinavians from across the Black Sea. They seized the Princes Islands, where the former patriarch Ignatius was being held, and carried off much booty, but later withdrew. The city's deliverance was ascribed to the Mother of God, and later stories about her intervention, much embroidered, found their way into the Russian twelfth-century *Primary Chronicle.* Photius delivered two homilies on the attack, with vivid accounts of the panic that had set in and the subsequent relief felt in Constantinople. Settling among Slavs, the Rus' acquired their language and their ways and not long after the attack in 860 they seem to have gained control of Kiev.

Christianization and influence went together. Byzantium had already been at work to Christianize the Slavs who had settled in Greece, and gave its blessing to Constantine and Methodius, two brothers from Thessalonike often referred to as the 'apostles to the Slavs'. A delegation from Moravia in 863 provided the opportunity. Frankish missionaries were also at work in central Europe promoting Latin Christianity, but Byzantium seems to have left Constantine and Methodius to their own devices. Their attempt to establish Christian worship in Slavonic did not prevent them from going to Rome and obtaining papal support. Constantine died and Methodius was sent by the pope to Pannonia, but then returned to Moravia, having encountered opposition from the Franks. He died in 885, the contest between

Slavonic and Latin rites still continuing. But although the mission had not fully succeeded, it led to the beginnings of Slav Christianity, the development of liturgy in Slavonic and a Slavonic law code based on Byzantine practice.

Byzantines and Bulgars

Bulgaria, ruled by the khan Boris, was also a site of competition for influence between westerners and Byzantines, and again Photius was involved. The Bulgars, originally a Turkic people who had migrated westwards, settled and become gradually Slavicized. Although they had adopted Greek in their administration, in 811 they inflicted a humiliating defeat on the Emperor Nicephorus I. Bulgaria remained a concern for Byzantine security and Michael III made a show of strength against them in 864 or 865, after which Boris was baptized by a Byzantine bishop. This provoked a revolt among his boyars that Boris was able to put down. Photius now sent a long and high-handed letter to Boris, setting out the essence of Byzantine Christianity and the duties of a Christian ruler. Not wanting to be strong-armed by Constantinople, Boris sent Pope Nicholas a list of 106 questions about the faith, mainly on practical issues such as fasting but also enquiring about the status of Constantinople and the other patriarchates. Its contents are known from Nicholas's more temperate reply, and the result was that Boris chose Rome. Photius then wrote another long letter of complaint to the eastern patriarchs, setting out the Byzantine objections to Latin Christianity, including its adoption of the *Filioque*. Soon after this he called the synod that excommunicated Nicholas, but was then deposed himself. In 870 a council was held in Constantinople to decide between the claims of Ignatius and Photius; it supported Ignatius. But it also ruled on which church the Bulgarians should adopt, and Boris now accepted its predictable decision in favour of Byzantium.

These episodes illustrate the ways accident, rivalry and politics were involved in the spread of Byzantine Christianity to other peoples. One can also see how the growing divide between the western and eastern churches played out in other geographical areas and how it has influenced the religious make-up of many countries today.

The Byzantine 'commonwealth'

One way of looking at the wider influence of Byzantium in this period is in terms of a 'commonwealth', the term used in a well-known book by Dimitri Obolensky (see 'Further reading' for this chapter). According to this view, Byzantium was at the heart of a commonwealth of nations, the mother civilization to which they looked. Christianity was a key component in this relationship. It has been argued that an earlier 'commonwealth' also existed around the eastern Mediterranean and the Caucasus, and, as we have seen, Byzantium saw the official adoption of Christianity as integral to broader political and diplomatic connections. In the longer term it was this 'commonwealth' that established Orthodoxy as the religion of much of eastern Europe and the Balkans, very much on the model of Christianity in Byzantium.

The Christianization of the Rus' is a case in point. The regent Olga visited Constantinople in the mid tenth century and was baptized, after which she tried to spread Christianity among the Rus'. It is, however, her grandson

Vladimir, prince of Kiev, who should have the credit, after allegedly investigating Latin Christianity, Judaism and Islam and choosing to convert to Orthodox Christianity in 988. Possibly also as a reward for helping the Emperor Basil to deal with a challenge to his throne, he was allowed to marry Basil's sister. Russian Orthodoxy traces its origins back to these events.

The idea of a benign commonwealth or family of nations was one that appealed to the Byzantines, in the sense that they always considered themselves the senior partner, and fostered the language of unequal but protective relationships. However, such terminology sees things from the Byzantine point of view and suggests an organizing principle that cannot be shown to have existed. A recent reformulation in terms of concentric circles of influence is more helpful, so long as it is remembered that Byzantine relations with other peoples were driven as much by opportunity and immediate need as by any wider or consistent aims. Byzantium saw things very much on its own terms. The tenth-century Emperor Constantine VII Porphyrogenitus ('born in the purple chamber' of the palace – see Chapter 7) drew up a work of guidance directed to his son Romanus in which he set out advice on the foreign policy and style of diplomacy to be used in dealing with the many neighbouring peoples to the north of Byzantium and beyond, as well as with the Pechenegs, Turks, Armenians and Georgians. The work gives advice for both diplomatic relations and direct rule, but it represents wishful thinking as much as real relationships.

Earlier in the tenth century, efforts were made by Byzantium to spread Christianity in the north Caucasus, and when envoys came from Hungary in the mid century, a newly consecrated bishop was sent back with them. Again, success was not immediate; moreover, Byzantine Christianity was often not the only kind among the peoples it reached, and Latin influences and religious competition in the Balkans and central Europe ensured a more complex religious scene.

Mount Athos and its monasteries

There had long been a monastic presence on Mount Athos (often known as the 'Holy Mountain'), a rocky peninsula jutting out into the Aegean Sea in north-east Greece. Like other mountainous sites, such as Mount Olympus in Bithynia, or indeed Sinai, it attracted both individuals and small groups who wanted to live a holy life. Its isolation is explained as an advantage by Athanasius, the tenth-century founder, under imperial instruction, of the Great Lavra, the first of the 20 or so monasteries on Mount Athos today, and set up by Athanasius with 80 monks. Athanasius's foundation was soon followed by a number of others, all still in existence today despite many vicissitudes in the intervening centuries. They included Georgian, Bulgarian, Russian and Serbian foundations and thus testify to the wider impact of Byzantine Christianity.

Mount Athos is unusual, indeed unique, in its concentration of large monasteries and their associated smaller settlements. From the tenth century onwards the Athos monasteries frequently benefited from imperial subsidies and favours, and by the late Byzantine period many had become wealthy landowners, especially in Thrace (northern Greece), with an extensive tied labour force; some even owned ships for trade. In 1320 the annual income of the

Great Lavra was calculated as 4,000 gold coins. Managing such resources was complex, and many documents survive recording their transactions, which brought them into contact and sometimes conflict with rich aristocratic families. Athanasius's tenth-century monastic rule, his *typikon*, or foundation document for the Great Lavra, and his testament (an updating of the rule), belong to a group of such surviving foundation documents for monasteries in Byzantium, each laying down the rule of life to be observed within the monastery. The monasteries on Mount Athos today have enjoyed something of a renaissance since the end of communism, with many monks arriving from eastern Europe. This international aspect, as well as the Athonite tradition itself, is the direct legacy of Byzantine Christianity.

7

The Macedonian emperors

Basil I (867–77) was the first of the Macedonian emperors, so-called because Basil came from the *theme*, or administrative district, of Macedonia in Thrace. The most notable emperors of this dynasty, which ruled until 1056, were Leo VI (886–912), Constantine VII (913–59, sole emperor 945–59) and Basil II (976–1025). In this period the empire was again ruled by a woman, or rather women: Zoe (1028–50), with her sister Theodora (1042). Zoe's third husband, Constantine Monomachus, ruled from 1042 to 1055, and Theodora ruled again from 1055 to 1056. During this period the empire also reached its largest point since before the Arab conquests. Bulgaria had been conquered earlier by Basil II (known as 'the Bulgar-slayer'), and Byzantium controlled south Italy and Dalmatia. The Rus' were forced back from Asia Minor, and Byzantium pushed into Mesopotamia and Syria and eventually recovered Crete and Cyprus. The Arabs had been successful in Sicily and Crete, and sacked Thessalonike in 904, and some of these Byzantine successes were hard won. Nevertheless the empire was on the offensive.

Leo VI ('Leo the Wise', 886–912)

Leo VI may have been the son of Michael III, whose reburial he ordered in the Church of the Holy Apostles. His reign was notable in several ways and he was an author himself, producing homilies, poems, orations and treatises. He was later credited with the so-called *Oracles of Leo the Wise*, a collection of material about divination and prophecy. Among the works that appeared during his reign, whether or not by Leo himself, was the *Taktika*, a treatise on military tactics. Two other important documents also date from his reign: the *Book of the Prefect*, which laid down detailed regulations for trades and crafts in Constantinople under the authority of the city prefect, and a listing of the officials and ranks at the court with their respective order of precedence. The system was highly organized, with offices and titles as well as military appointments carrying stipends from the state; as such they were highly desirable, and offices and titles could be purchased. An elaborate court ceremonial reinforced these hierarchies, as we know from the *Book of Ceremonies* compiled under Leo's son and successor (below), and church dignitaries occupied prominent places in imperial protocols. Many of the ceremonies laid down also involved imperial participation in religious services and processions. Finally, Leo set up a legal commission to revise Justinian's codification of Roman law; it produced the *Basilika*, in Greek rather than Justinian's Latin, and incorporated ecclesiastical as well as secular law. Leo's own laws were known as *Novels* ('new laws'), following another precedent set by Justinian.

Leo was less successful in his military operations, and he met with major opposition from the Church, and especially from the then patriarch, when he proposed after three marriages had failed to produce a male heir to marry his mistress, who had given birth to a son. This dispute is what is known as the Tetragamy, or 'Fourth marriage' crisis. Leo deposed the patriarch and the marriage was allowed, but the emperor was subjected to a heavy penance. One of Leo's opponents was the learned Arethas, metropolitan of Caesarea, a commentator and collector of classical texts and the most prominent scholar of the day.

Constantine VII Porphyrogenitus
(905–59, sole emperor 945–59)

The son born to Leo and his mistress Zoe Karbonopsina was Constantine VII Porphyrogenitus. Despite being made co-emperor by his father, his position was insecure and he did not become sole emperor until 945. Nevertheless he presided over an impressive and important collection of writings: they include the *Book of Ceremonies*, a collection of protocols for imperial ceremonies addressed to his son, already mentioned, the treatise *On the Administration of the Empire*, a continuation of the early ninth-century chronicle of Theophanes, a work *On the Themes*, on the geography of the empire, a *Life* of the Emperor Basil, justifying the rise of the Macedonian dynasty, and finally, collections of classified excerpts from classical historians.

The arts also flourished, in what has somewhat misleadingly been called the Macedonian renaissance. Ivories, icon painting and metalwork show a high technical standard and a more naturalistic style. This was a high point in terms of the workings of the Byzantine state, and the splendour of the court made a lasting impression, both positive and negative, on the western bishop Liutprand of Cremona, who was sent on two missions to Constantinople in 949 and 968 and described his reactions in vivid detail.

In 944, the year before Constantine VII became sole emperor, a great event took place in Constantinople with the 'translation', or arrival, of the Mandylion or Image of Edessa, removed from Edessa in Mesopotamia (see Chapter 3) by the successful Byzantine general John Kourkouas. This image of Christ's face (now lost), believed to have been miraculously imprinted on a cloth, became one of the most sacred objects in Constantinople, where it joined relics of the Passion of Christ in the Pharos chapel in the imperial palace. Many Orthodox churches today have depictions of the Image of Edessa as part of their decoration.

It was during the reign of Constantine VII that Olga of Kiev visited Constantinople (see Chapter 6). Constantine's generals were also active against the Arabs on the eastern frontier, with successes on the Euphrates and especially in northern Syria under Nicephorus Phocas, who became emperor himself in 963 when Constantine VII's son Romanus died at an early age.

Basil II (976–1025), a warrior emperor

These were expansionist days. Unlike Constantine VII, Basil II took the field himself and was able to put down a revolt by rivals in Anatolia, helped by his alliance with Vladimir of Kiev. When a truce made with the Fatimids failed, Basil forced them to retreat from Aleppo in 995. Byzantine armies were in Syria and in what is now Lebanon until 1000, when another truce was made, this time for ten years, and Basil turned his attention elsewhere. Nine years later the Fatimid caliph al-Hakim bi-Amr Allah's anti-Christian activities led to serious damage being done to the Church of the Holy Sepulchre in Jerusalem. It was restored, though not completely, at great expense under the Emperor Constantine IX Monomachus, husband of the Empress Zoe, as a result of an agreement with al-Hakim's successor, and a patriarch was reappointed. Byzantium thus reasserted its historic connection with Jerusalem and the holy places.

Basil is best known for his conquest and annexation of Bulgaria, which extended from the Black Sea to the Adriatic, for which he later acquired the legendary title of 'Bulgar-slayer'. The campaigns against Samuel, the expansionist ruler of Bulgaria, lasted from 1000 to 1018, and again the emperor himself led his troops and won considerable successes. After his victory at the Kleidion pass in 1014 he is said to have taken thousands of prisoners and blinded huge numbers of them. Bulgaria was organized into an ecclesiastical as well as an administrative province, and Byzantine clergy and the Greek language introduced; we know a good deal about how this did and did not work from the letters of Theophylact, who became Archbishop of Ochrid late in the eleventh century.

Symeon the New Theologian

Symeon (d. 1022) was a controversial ascetic figure who spent a long period as abbot of the Saint Mamas monastery in Constantinople but provoked opposition from the church authorities and his own monks for his teachings and his perceived extremism. He is known for his highly personal writings and his teachings about the divine light and direct experience of God. He carried to new lengths the earlier traditions of asceticism, mysticism and inwardness. Symeon provoked suspicion in his own day but, however personal and outspoken, his teachings and his writings placed him in the long tradition of hesychasm ('quietness' before God) that stretched from the Desert Fathers onwards and was later identified with Gregory Palamas (see Chapter 10), and which is reflected in the later ascetic compilation known as the *Philokalia* (see Chapter 11).

1054: the 'Great Schism'

The world around Byzantium was changing and becoming more complex. The Normans had arrived in south Italy in the eleventh century, and difficulties soon arose about the differences between Latin and Byzantine Christianity. There were many Orthodox Christians in south Italy and one of the irritants that soon arose was over the western use of unleavened bread (*azymes*) in the Eucharist, which seemed to the Greeks to hint of Judaism. The Archbishop of Ochrid at the time complained about it, and Latin churches in Constantinople were imprudently closed. Again two formidable personages clashed. This time it was Cardinal Humbert, who was sent to Constantinople as a papal legate to protest, and Michael Cerularius, the patriarch of Constantinople, who were involved.

In his response to Leo of Ochrid, Humbert mounted an aggressive and detailed attack on eastern practice. But hostility had also been mounting in Constantinople: Humbert impugned Cerularius's elevation to the patriarchate and Cerularius was suspicious of the papal legation. Although the emperor was more inclined to conciliation, hoping for papal support against the Normans in Italy, feelings were inflamed. But the exasperated Humbert went further: in July 1054 he laid a papal bull of excommunication against Cerularius on the altar during the liturgy in Hagia Sophia, despite the fact that the pope had already died and Humbert was acting ultra vires. This was too much. The emperor allowed Cerularius to anathematize Humbert and the Roman legation and to burn the Greek translation of the Latin bull.

A great deal has been written about this clash. It is often referred to as 'the Great Schism', after which it is held that the western and eastern churches were divided. The reality was far more complex. Humbert was certainly unnecessarily provocative, but his excommunication was personal rather than representing the beginning of a formal break with the whole eastern Church. Indeed, he later tried to enlist the support of the other eastern patriarchs. Not all Byzantines agreed with Cerularius, and no profound consequences followed, even though in the centuries to come an endless stream of polemical treatises and other works was produced on both sides. The differences remained, not only about the *Filioque* and the question of Roman primacy but also in many other issues of practice, including clerical celibacy (practised in the west but not in Byzantium except for bishops) and the fact that western clergy, unlike the Byzantines, were clean-shaven – the list expanded as time went on. Other factors were also relevant. The eleventh century was the period of papal reform and the successful assertion of papal prerogatives under Gregory VII in relation to the Holy Roman Empire and other western powers, both developments that were potentially difficult for east–west relations.

In later periods Byzantines needed papal and western support and made strenuous efforts to achieve union. More papal legations were sent to Constantinople, and some later emperors were inclined to favour the Roman side. But the Byzantines themselves were divided. The Councils of Lyons (1274) and Ferrara/Florence (1438–9) each ended in agreement to union. In the aftermath of the latter, several of the senior Byzantine delegates converted to Roman Catholicism and were raised to high positions in the Roman Church. But there was also strong opposition to union in Byzantium both then and after the earlier Council of Lyons.

The disputes with the Latins that came to a head under Photius and resurfaced later were further intensified with the advent of the Crusades at the end of the eleventh century. They became the backdrop against which Byzantine foreign relations as well as ecclesiastical life were played out until the end of the Byzantine period.

8

Byzantium under the Comneni

In 1071, Byzantium suffered two major blows: a crushing defeat from the Seljuk Turks at Manzikert in eastern Turkey, in which the Emperor Romanus IV Diogenes was captured, and the capture by the Normans of Bari, the main Byzantine centre in south Italy. The expansionism of the tenth century came to a sudden end, and again Byzantium was threatened by external developments and changes in the political and military situation. During the tenth century some landowning families in Anatolia were becoming powerful enough to challenge imperial authority, and it was from this background that Alexius I Comnenus was able to seize the throne in 1081.

Alexius ruled from 1081 until 1118, and we know most about his reign from the flattering history written by his daughter Anna, the only female Byzantine historian, though other Byzantine writers saw him very differently. Alexius's mother, Anna Dalassena, and the previous empress, Maria of Alania, were also prominent and forceful imperial women, and both were instrumental in his seizure of the throne. Anna was disappointed when an attempt to ensure the succession after Alexius for her husband Nicephorus Bryennius failed, and in her history she defends her father's reputation and presents him as a glorious emperor. He was certainly faced with some serious problems. The empire was now threatened on three sides: by the advance of the

Seljuks in Anatolia; the Normans in south Italy and across the Adriatic; and the Pechenegs and then the Cumans (who had fought with the Byzantines against the Pechenegs) in Thrace. It seems that the Pechenegs were aided by Paulicians and Bogomils, dualist heretics, some serving in the Byzantine armies. Alexius had been a general before he came to the throne and he now led his armies with varying success, winning some decisive battles but also employing diplomatic means when he could. He was still campaigning against the Seljuks in the last years of his life.

All this put great pressure on the Byzantine army, and Alexius made extensive use of mercenaries. He also discontinued the silver coinage and introduced a new gold coin, the *hyperpyron*. He gave preference to the aristocratic families, to which he himself belonged, and established a new system of titles and dignities for the extended imperial family; this was the age of a new kind of Byzantine aristocracy, tied by connections of kinship to the emperor, a system that Alexius hoped would bind the great families to the state and reduce their capacity for rebellion. But in order to pay for his campaigns Alexius needed more tax revenue, and resorted to sequestering ecclesiastical treasures, a policy that was hotly contested.

Alexius also presented himself as the defender of orthodoxy against the dangers of heresy. Early in his reign John Italus ('the Italian', from Calabria in south Italy), a prominent philosopher, teacher and author of expositions of Aristotle, was tried and sent to a monastery for offences including allegedly promoting the teachings of Plato. A lengthy condemnation of his heretical teachings was added to the Synodicon of Orthodoxy (see Chapter 3). Others were also condemned for their views during Alexius's reign, including Eustratius, Bishop of Nicaea, whose downfall was claimed to have been connected with his predilection for Aristotelian logic. John Italus was allowed to retract his teachings, but much later in Alexius's reign – though it is hard to disentangle what happened from Anna's highly coloured account – a certain Basil, an alleged leader of the Bogomil dualists, was publicly burned in the hippodrome in Constantinople in an unusually extreme display of anti-heretical zeal. Alexius also commissioned a vast encyclopaedic work condemning Bogomilism and setting out the other heresies that were held to threaten orthodox belief, together with their refutations; it included a chapter on Islam, regarded as a Christian heresy by Byzantine writers since John of Damascus. All Byzantine emperors were formally acclaimed as orthodox by the court and population on public occasions, whatever their actual position, but Alexius made a special point of underlining his imperial authority by presenting himself in this way.

The First Crusade

Yet again Byzantium was confronted with an unexpected issue from outside its borders, this time in the shape of the Crusades. Alexius was conscious of the need for good relations with the papacy, even though there were by now two rival popes. However, his request to Pope Urban II for assistance in his campaigns against the Seljuk Turks in 1095, debated in a council in Piacenza, was followed only months later by the same Pope Urban's call for the First Crusade at Clermont. Alexius now had to deal with a procession of westerners passing through his lands on their way to the Holy Land, and Anna gives a vivid account of the arrival of their leaders when they reached Constantinople: they seemed in her eyes uncouth, yet at the same time strangely impressive.

Accounts of the Crusade in western sources differ sharply from eastern ones, and lay emphasis on the duplicity of the Byzantines. In fact Alexius successfully turned the situation to his advantage, and was able to recover much territory lost to the Seljuks. He made the Crusader leaders swear oaths of homage and promise to restore conquered lands to Byzantium. When the Norman Bohemond led his troops against Alexius, the emperor was able to compel him to surrender and acknowledge his authority. The Crusaders would return to change the pattern of settlement and authority in the Holy Land and the east, but for now Alexius's policy had paid off.

Manuel I (1143–80)

Despite the efforts to replace him with Anna's husband Nicephorus Bryennius, Alexius's son John became emperor from 1118 to 1143 and was successful as a military ruler, with victories in the Balkans over the Pechenegs, Hungarians and Serbs, and considerable success in regaining territory from the Seljuks in the east. However, his further expedition against the Muslims as far to the east as Syria exposed the unreliability of the Crusaders as Byzantine allies when an agreement to hand over Antioch to the Byzantines failed. A plan to make a pilgrimage to Crusader-held Jerusalem also came to nothing and John died before he could recover Antioch. The empire's reach was now greatly extended, but it had to face new enemies and rivals and an external situation that was becoming ever more complex.

These were the conditions inherited in 1143 by Manuel I, John's younger son and his chosen heir. Manuel was a highly active emperor on several fronts and his long reign allowed a cultural flowering among literary figures and intellectuals, as well as engagement with Latins and others on theological matters. Among the Italian trading cities, Venice had been granted a concession in Constantinople, and was soon followed by Pisa and Genoa. In Manuel's day there were numerous Latins living in designated areas in the city, as well as several embassies arriving from the papacy, and the emperor was seen as pro-unionist. He followed Alexius's example in commissioning a further encyclopaedic work addressing heresies, and recounting the debates between himself and a group of Roman cardinals about Roman primacy and the *Filioque*, and between himself and the Armenians. Both dialogues were reinforced by long lists of patristic citations, and not for nothing was this work known as 'The Sacred Armoury'. Manuel himself was well trained in argumentation, including Aristotelian logic, and he was also determined. He took a high view of his own role in relation to the Church and debated with the patriarch Nicholas Mouzalon, arguing that the latter's election was irregular, as well as forcing the synod to accept a pro-Latin interpretation of a key Gospel text (John 14.28, 'the Father is greater than I'), and sending a delegate armed with large numbers of books to debate on theology with the head of the Armenian church. In his debates with the Latins, Manuel drew on the assistance of Hugh Eteriano, a Pisan lay theologian living in Constantinople, who was a supporter of Pope Alexander III and had studied Aristotle in Paris. Among his other services, Manuel commissioned from Eteriano a work setting out the Latin position on the Holy Spirit and the Trinity on the basis of Greek authorities.

Under Manuel I, poetry and rhetoric flourished, and intellectuals and schools competed against each other over teaching positions and patronage. These schools were for higher-level students, and mainly taught rhetoric, as part of the Greek *paideia*, the higher education without which neither a public career nor advanced ecclesiastical positions were possible. For the first time it became possible to earn one's living by literary skill, and the literary output of the period, which included the revival of the Greek 'novel', with stories of adventure and romantic love, makes it one of the most brilliant in Byzantium's history. Leading churchmen were themselves highly educated in the secular classics and able to write in high literary style. Letters and history writing flourished and classical texts were read, studied and edited. A few aristocratic women were also highly educated and became literary patrons. However, the majority of the population had little access to more than the lower levels of education, if that. Moreover, there had long been an increasing divide between the high-style Greek of the educated elite and the ordinary spoken Greek, and this intensified as the literary culture of the elite became even more rarefied.

Like his grandfather Alexius I, Manuel had to deal with Crusaders as the Second Crusade, led by the kings Louis III of France and Conrad III of Germany, crossed Byzantine territory in 1147 on its way to the east. Manuel was cautious. Byzantium was less interested in joining in the Crusade than in fending off the Crusaders, and when the German contingent arrived outside Constantinople there were clashes with Byzantine forces; Manuel's dealings with the French contingent also led to rancour. The Crusade was unsuccessful, and Saladin's victory at Hattin in 1187 led to his siege and capture of Jerusalem.

After Manuel I: things go wrong

The years after Manuel I's death in 1180 were much less stable, and Byzantine hostility to the Latins increased to the point where Latins in Constantinople were attacked and many killed. The last Comnenian emperor, Andronicus I Comnenus, had had a colourful past, first as a captive of the Seljuk Turks and then as a fugitive at the courts of the prince of Antioch, King Amalric of Jerusalem and Nur-ad-Din, sultan of Damascus. He became the husband in turn of Theodora Comnena, the widow of Baldwin III, and Agnes of France, still a child at the time. His reign was short and brutal: he attacked his powerful aristocratic rivals, but his excesses led to a Norman invasion mounted from Sicily and he was deposed, mutilated and killed in the Hippodrome in Constantinople late in 1185.

Constantinople falls to the Fourth Crusade

The family-centred system initiated by Alexius I did not succeed in removing these internal dangers, and the situation deteriorated further as the end of the twelfth century approached. The Fourth Crusade was launched by Pope Innocent III in 1202 and the Crusader fleet approached Constantinople in 1203, deflected from its original destination of Egypt. The Crusaders initially supported the usurper Alexius III Angelus on the basis of promises of payments, but the usurpation failed. A confused series of events followed in which Byzantine forces were found wanting but also successfully repelled an attack on the city's fortifications. In 1204 the Crusaders, urged on by their own clergy, attacked Constantinople, with the Venetian fleet playing a central role. The capture and sack of Constantinople by the Fourth Crusade and the looting of its treasures, including its most sacred relics (see Chapter 9), represented the most tragic event in its history before the city's final capture in 1453.

9

1204 and after

The world of Byzantium now changed dramatically. For nearly six decades, until 1261, the Byzantines were driven into exile and the Byzantine empire was parcelled out between Venice and its allies, while Constantinople was ruled by a Latin emperor with a Latin patriarch. A period of fragmentation followed as the once extensive empire broke up into a number of small enclaves. Although the Byzantine court and administration were re-established in Constantinople in 1261 and the Palaeologan dynasty (see Chapter 10) remained on the throne until 1453, the lands they ruled were tiny in comparison with the empire of the Comneni. By 1453 only a very small population remained in the capital, amid gardens and deserted buildings. Lesser Byzantine princedoms ruled elsewhere, at Mistra in the Peloponnese and in Epirus; Thessalonike had fallen to the Ottomans more than 20 years before. A Byzantine 'empire' was founded at Trebizond on the north coast of modern Turkey but surrendered to the Ottomans in 1461.

Nevertheless, and perhaps paradoxically, the last centuries of Byzantium constituted one of its most memorable periods in cultural terms. Theodore I Laskaris fled from Constantinople to Nicaea in western Asia Minor and was able to fend off the Normans and his rivals and to establish a Byzantine court in exile at Nicaea, with a Byzantine patriarch and many of the familiar trappings of Byzantine rule.

A continuity of language, culture, ideology and religious values thus linked pre-1204 Constantinople with the re-established Byzantine Constantinople of 1261 onwards. Meanwhile the world outside had changed dramatically, with far more fragmentation and rival groups and polities in the eastern Mediterranean. It would be wrong to imagine that this was not reflected in the lives of the Byzantine elites themselves, and they were increasingly affected by inter-marriage and the adoption of western customs. Nevertheless they also clung with dogged persistence to what they saw as their own identity, and continued to do so against what at times seemed enormous odds.

1204: the sack of Constantinople

Constantinople had already been severely damaged by fires in 1203 and early 1204, whether set by the Crusaders or resulting from Byzantine anti-Latin rioting, and the events of the capture and sack in April 1204 are described in vivid detail by both westerners and Byzantines, most vividly and emotionally by a Byzantine eyewitness, Nicetas Choniates. Choniates held one of the high positions in the adminis-tration and when the Crusaders attacked he had already reached the year 1202 in his *History* of the imperial reigns starting from the death of Alexius I Comnenus in 1118; he worked on his account of the sack and also revised his *History* after he and his family had fled from the city. He also wrote an account of the treasures looted by the Crusaders, which included many classical statues. His own experience features prominently in his account of the capture; during the sack he lost his own house near Hagia Sophia and all his library, and was witness to many tragic incidents. He went on to record the difficulties he experienced after leaving the city and after he reached Nicaea. He asked himself who was to blame for what had happened, and did not spare the feebleness of the Byzantines or the catastrophic effect of the flight of the Emperor Alexius III. Choniates's brother, Michael, was the metropolitan of Athens, and the *History* covered contemporary doctrinal disputes as well as political narrative. Choniates also composed the *Dogmatic Panoply*, a third huge compendium against heresies in the manner of those compiled earlier under Alexius I and Manuel I, with a title conceived along similar lines.

The capture of Constantinople enabled the Crusaders to seize huge amounts of booty, including the city's most precious relics and church treasures. Many can still be seen in the treasury of San Marco in Venice, where the Pala d'Oro altarpiece incorporates Byzantine enamels. Particularly striking is the Byzantine icon of the Virgin of Victory (*Nikopoia*). The crown of thorns from the Passion of Christ, pawned and then redeemed by the Latins in the aftermath of the sack, is in Notre Dame in Paris. The Image of Edessa was also housed in Paris in the Sainte Chapelle, but lost with other treasures during the French Revolution. Many others were more widely dispersed in the unseemly rush to acquire them.

The Byzantine experience of 1204 led to intense bitterness against the Latins, which became an intensifying factor in the hostile attitudes to the western Church. In 1214 the metropolitan of Cyzicus in Asia Minor wrote a blistering attack on the Latins, focusing on the issues of papal primacy and the Crusading concept of holy war: Latin clergy and bishops had urged on the sack of Constantinople and taken part themselves. The capture of Constantinople, and the

Latin empire that followed, also had profound and lasting consequences in many other spheres. The Byzantine emperor was now driven from Constantinople and Byzantine government was reduced to a few small areas. The political map of the Mediterranean changed dramatically. Though there was a Byzantine return to Constantinople in 1261 there could be no return to the previous imperial reach.

The Latin empire and Romania

After the capture and sack of Constantinople, Baldwin of Flanders became Latin emperor and the influence of Venice prevailed. Byzantine territory further afield, known as Romania to the westerners, had already been shared out between the future emperor, Venice and the other Crusaders. However, the reality was messier than this suggests and in practice the Latin 'empire' could not control very much. Baldwin was crowned in Hagia Sophia by a new Latin patriarch, the Venetian Thomas Morosini, and was soon recognized by Pope Innocent III, but his powers were limited and constrained by the other Crusader barons. Though some of the trappings of the Byzantine court were retained, the Latin emperor was a pale shadow of his Byzantine predecessors. The Venetian administration was based at the monastery of the Pantokrator, to which the icon of the Virgin Hodegetria was moved from Hagia Sophia. The new relationships were expressed in western terms of fealty, but Venice had to struggle to assert control in its theoretical gains outside the capital.

The Latin empire was weak from the start. Only a year after the sack of Constantinople the Latins were heavily defeated by the Bulgarians at Adrianople and Baldwin himself was captured; they were also faced by military threats from Epirus and Nicaea. It was after a successful campaign by a general from Nicaea that Michael Palaeologus was able to enter Constantinople in 1261 and declare himself Michael VIII; he did not even have to conquer the city himself.

Innocent III was a powerful pope and the Fourth Lateran Council, called by him in 1215, is regarded as a landmark in the history of papal reform. He had already wrestled with the question of how much leeway could be allowed to the eastern Christians and at first tried to impose the Latin rite on them. But by 1215 a Latinizing policy already seemed less feasible and the council was prepared to be more accommodating. Nevertheless local conditions varied greatly. Within Constantinople many churches and monasteries were taken over by the Latins, with some liturgical rearrangements, and Franciscans, Benedictines, Cistercians and Dominicans became established in the city. Many churches lost the revenues they had derived from donations and land holdings and others fell into disrepair and were plundered. Church organization along Latin lines in Constantinople did not last. But elsewhere, in the Aegean islands and other former Byzantine territories, the mixture of Latin and Greek brought lasting complications.

The 'empire' of Nicaea

Nicaea, a small but historic city with impressive walls, was now the seat of Byzantine administration. Latin forces were dangerously near at Nicomedia but by relying on mercenaries, Theodore I Laskaris was able to field an army and to mint coins further south at Magnesia. His son-in-law and successor was John III Vatatzes, a successful emperor whose second wife was the daughter of the German Emperor Frederick II, and who made his base partly there and partly at Nymphaion, while Nicaea remained the official centre and the seat of the patriarch. Under terms agreed with the Latins, more Byzantines were allowed to leave Constantinople, and trade and travel between the two cities remained possible.

Small though Nicaea was, Byzantine intellectual life was maintained. Theodore II, the son of Vatatzes, was an accomplished rhetorician and set up an imperial school of rhetoric and poetics. Choniates had found his transplantation there difficult, but Nicaea was home to two other major writers, Nicholas Mesarites and Nicephorus Blemmydes. The former had been a cleric of Hagia Sophia and became Bishop of Ephesus; he was appointed to discuss union with a papal embassy in Constantinople, in one of several such sets of discussions with the Byzantines at Nicaea. Blemmydes was a scholar and writer and a member of the patriarchal clergy; he was employed on missions to seek out dualists in Asia Minor and took part in theological debates with Latin envoys. Theodore I Laskaris had also occupied himself with internal doctrinal issues, including the interpretation of John 14.28, 'the Father is greater than I', which had been a major issue under Manuel I (see Chapter 8), and life at Nicaea was punctuated by synods and embassies just as it had been in Constantinople.

Relations between Nicaea and Epirus were not straightforward, and the empire of Nicaea was faced with rivalry both ecclesiastical and military. When Theodore Comnenus Doukas of Epirus was crowned as emperor at Thessalonike in the 1220s, the patriarch at Nicaea complained and Nicaea eventually prevailed. The Bulgarians posed another major threat, but a matrimonial alliance under John Vatatzes allowed the Byzantines of Nicaea to get a foothold in Thrace. The Seljuks were ensconced in Anatolia, but relations were not all bad, and the Byzantines at Nicaea profited from trade with them. Given the confused situation, they were also able to appropriate estates in Anatolia, and John Vatatzes took measures to streamline the taxation and fiscal system. He was even able to support restoration work in Constantinople at the churches of Blachernae, the Holy Apostles and elsewhere.

A fragmented world

Western immigration into Romania helped to establish the Latin presence, but the Latins were not united and there was no likelihood of their establishing Latin rule over the entire former Byzantine territory. In its place a patchwork of large and small political entities with loose or no connections with each other evolved in the islands and on the European side. In the Peloponnese, Franks were granted fiefdoms and the local Greek population reduced to second-class status. Trade and markets were reorientated on a new axis, stimulated by western demand. The Seljuks were defeated by the Mongols in the 1240s but the Byzantines at Nicaea were successful in fending off the threat and this continued under Michael VIII after 1261. But by the end of the century Asia Minor was lost. Byzantium now existed in a very different world.

10

Byzantium 1261–1453

Michael Palaeologus knew how to stage an entry. On 15 August 1261, the most important feast day of the Virgin, he entered the city on foot through the Golden Gate, preceded by the icon of the Virgin Hodegetria that the Venetians had removed from Hagia Sophia. Although he had already been crowned as co-emperor, he was now crowned again in Hagia Sophia. But Michael had usurped the throne, and on Christmas Day of the same year, on another very deliberately chosen day, he had the only surviving heir to the Laskarid dynasty of Nicaea blinded.

This action caused many problems for him. Michael was excommunicated by the patriarch Arsenius, who was eventually replaced by Joseph. But when under threat from Charles of Anjou in 1273 Michael sought union with the Latin Church, Joseph retired to a monastery rather than attend the proposed council, and later resigned. His successor, John Bekkos, imprisoned in 1273, now changed sides and argued for the union that resulted from the Council of Lyons in 1274, when the small Byzantine delegation to the council had accepted the *Filioque* and pledged safe passage for a new Crusade to the Holy Land. After Michael's death in 1282, Bekkos was deposed in turn by Michael's son Andronicus II, who reversed the unionist policy; he was later exiled and imprisoned again.

Michael's immediate task was to re-establish the Byzantine administration in Constantinople and to assess the rebuilding needs in the city after nearly 60 years of Latin rule. In addition to the damage done in the fires of 1203 and 1204 and during the capture, many buildings had been taken over by the Latins in the following decades, including churches and monasteries, and others had become neglected and derelict. There were also abandoned areas within the city, and in the words of a later Byzantine writer, it was 'a plain of desolation'. The walls were a priority; both the Blachernae palace and the old Great Palace were in a bad state, and Hagia Sophia had had to be restored to Byzantine liturgical use in time for the emperor's coronation. Michael even built a new mosque, seemingly in the context of an agreement with the Mamluks of Egypt, now the major Muslim power in the eastern Mediterranean. Church restoration was seen as an urgent need, and in addition houses had to be assigned to members of the Byzantine elite who had come from Nicaea. Michael was proud of his achievements: Byzantine writers tell us that he commissioned a column in front of the church of the Holy Apostles, topped by the archangel Michael, with the emperor himself kneeling and offering his restored city.

Byzantium surrounded

The recovery of Constantinople came about through a combination of luck and Latin weakness. But the Byzantines were exposed to a multitude of threats and also chronically short of funds to meet them. So severe was their need that at the end of the fourteenth century, while Constantinople was under siege by the Ottoman Sultan Bayezid I, the Emperor Manuel II left on an extended tour of Europe trying to raise funds, and spent Christmas 1400 as the guest of King Henry IV at Eltham Palace outside London. Yet the Byzantines managed to hang on for nearly two centuries. There was wealth in private hands and in some of the Athonite monasteries; it came above all from trade and from the new trading networks and markets that had opened up in the Mediterranean.

After Michael's return in 1261, Constantinople was threatened, from Bulgaria, by the Mongols, who dominated Anatolia and had taken Aleppo and Damascus, and by the Latins; the Genoese, Michael's allies, were defeated by the Venetians. The Byzantine Despotate of Epirus was also unfriendly, and Charles of Anjou, King of Sicily and Naples, represented a serious danger. Michael needed allies, not least against a further threat from Hungary, and marriage alliances were also useful. But while there were new commercial opportunities, the Byzantine world was now fragmented and dangerous. A new threat presented itself from the rise of the Ottomans. In the course of the fourteenth century they took Adrianople (Edirne), occupied Thessalonike (1387) and defeated the Serbs and others at the Battle of Kosovo (1389). The Byzantine emperor became their vassal, and before his accession in 1391 the future Emperor Manuel II Palaeologus spent several months as a hostage at the Ottoman court in Ankara. It was in the context of an Ottoman siege of Constantinople that began in 1394 and lasted until 1402 that he left to seek assistance from European rulers. In 1421 the Ottomans besieged Constantinople and Thessalonike, and Thessalonike, then held by the Venetians, fell in 1430.

Constantinople and Thessalonike in the fourteenth century

The ties between Constantinople and Thessalonike during this period were close, and Manuel II had been governor of Thessalonike himself. The two cities also shared a vigorous intellectual life, with teachers and writers moving from one to the other. But Thessalonike had had a turbulent history. Controlled by Epirus and then by Bulgaria and recovered by Nicaea, in the 1340s it was the site of bitter internal strife and social unrest, complicated by the ramifications of a civil war raging in Constantinople stirred up against the Emperor John VI Cantacuzene by the regents for the young John V Palaeologus, who turned for help first to Stephen Dušan of Serbia and then to the Turks in Bursa. Meanwhile in 1347, Gregory Palamas, a monk of Mount Athos and one of the greatest Byzantine theologians, was elected Archbishop of Thessalonike. Palamas was strongly supported by John VI Cantacuzene and had been imprisoned by the latter's rivals. He had already engaged in theological argument with Barlaam of Calabria, defending the Athonite tradition of spirituality against Barlaam's objections. Palamas was supported by the monks of Athos, but the argument was very divisive and it took a series of synods held in Constantinople between 1341 and 1351 to decide in Palamas's favour. Palamas was no enemy of Aristotelian logic, and also drew on Augustine, but his teachings are mainly identified with hesychasm ('quietness'), and insisted on the need for prayer and the technique of prayer focusing on the Jesus Prayer or Prayer of the Heart ('Lord Jesus Christ, son of God, have mercy on me, a sinner'). They became basic to the eastern Church, but this did not happen without difficulty, or immediately. In 1354 Palamas was captured by pirates and held at the Ottoman court until he was ransomed, while in the same year John VI was ousted and became a monk, and engaged in writing the history of his own times. This was a critical period for Byzantine theology, when Greek translations were also made of Thomas Aquinas's *Summa contra Gentiles* and of Latin polemical writings against Islam, and Constantinople itself was also home to Dominicans and Franciscans.

A cultural flowering

Literature and scholarship flourished under the Palaeologan dynasty, and this was also a period notable for its highly educated female patrons, some of whom also founded monasteries. Intellectuals set a high value on the works of classical authors, which they also collected and edited. Some, like Bessarion, built up major collections of manuscripts, and the arrival of many of these manuscripts in Italy before and after 1453 was a major factor in the rediscovery of classical learning in the Renaissance.

A distinctive architectural style can be seen in the buildings of this era, with banded brickwork and tall domes, and many of these were the result of private patronage. In Thessalonike the churches of the Holy Apostles and of the prophet Elijah, and the Vlatadon monastery, all belong to this period. Arta in northern Greece, which became the centre of the Despotate of Epirus, is also rich in late Byzantine churches. The early fourteenth-century additions to the Chora monastery in Constantinople (Turkish Kariye Djami) are attributable to the patronage of the statesman and scholar Theodore Metochites and constitute some of the finest and most beautiful mosaics and frescoes in the whole of Byzantine art. Metochites himself is depicted wearing a large turban, offering a model of his church to Christ, and the frescoes have a subtle naturalistic style that points towards the Renaissance. Among those who taught at the Chora monastery was the great scholar and commentator on classical texts, Maximus Planoudes, and Nicephorus Gregoras, the historian, scholar and opponent of Palamas, was confined there when he refused to retract after the council of 1351.

This was – at elite level – a highly literary and learned society that prized scholarship and classical learning. Greek was already being taught in Florence, and Byzantine exiles after 1453 brought with them Greek manuscripts and access to classical learning. The question must arise of how far the developments of the Renaissance were prefigured in Palaeologan culture, but Byzantium was very different from the Italian city states. Furthermore Byzantine promise was abruptly cut short. The cultural flowering of the Palaeologan period remains remarkable but the rise of schools and universities, and the advent of scholasticism in the Latin west, had no parallels in Byzantium.

Mistra, the Council of Ferrara/Florence and its antecedents

Like Constantinople, Mistra was a home of intellectual activity in the late Palaeologan period. Its most important scholar and teacher was George Gemistus Plethon, whose students included the future Cardinal Bessarion and George Scholarius, who became Orthodox patriarch under the Ottomans after the conquest of Constantinople (see

Chapter 14). Plethon was a passionate admirer of Plato and advocated the organization of society along Platonic lines. His work *On the Laws*, based on Plato's dialogue of the same title, was later burned as pagan and heretical. That Plethon was a pagan himself seems unlikely, however. He was part of the Byzantine delegation to the Council of Ferrara/Florence (1438–9) and defended the Byzantine position, though he also spread the knowledge of Plato in Florence and is claimed to have influenced Cosimo de' Medici. The large Byzantine delegation to the council headed by the Emperor John VIII Palaeologus spent many months in Italy and there were ample opportunities for the Greeks while there to experience the atmosphere of the early Renaissance. After the council Bessarion was not the only Byzantine to settle in Italy, where he became a Roman Catholic cardinal, supported Greek exiles and promoted Greek scholarship; his collection of manuscripts formed the basis of the Biblioteca Marciana in Venice.

Despite the hostile reception given to the result of the Council of Lyons in 1274, union between the Latin and Greek churches remained a major concern, now complicated by western debates about the status of councils and the fact that from 1378 to 1415 there were two rival popes. A council was called in Basel to defend the status of councils against popes. John, Bishop of Ragusa and a Dominican theologian, armed himself for future theological debate by buying as many books as he could from Constantinople. Pope Eugenius IV responded by calling a rival council to be held in Ferrara in 1438, and the Byzantine emperor, who travelled via Venice with a very large retinue, chose to go to Ferrara rather than Basel. The council agenda included discussions about the western doctrine of purgatory but

77

was dominated by the issue of the *Filioque*; agreeing to papal primacy was the second essential for union. Plague in Ferrara prompted a move to Florence early in 1439 and by July agreement was reached on union, under pressure from the Emperor John VIII, who was desperate for western help against the Ottoman threat to Constantinople. Many Byzantines already thought better of it while still on the return journey.

The Ottoman conquest of Constantinople

The Council of Ferrara/Florence thus led to division at home, and the agreed Crusade against the Ottomans was defeated at Varna in 1444. When Mehmet II succeeded his father as sultan in 1451 he began preparing for a decisive attack on Constantinople. The building of the great Ottoman fortress of Rumeli Hisar facing its twin, Anadolu Hisar, on the other side of the Bosphorus was the prelude to a siege beginning in April 1453. The city fell on 29 May; Mehmet rode his horse into Hagia Sophia and allowed three days of looting. The Emperor Constantine XI Palaeologus was killed, but strangely his body was not identified and according to legend he was turned to marble and placed by an angel in a cave from which he would one day return to save the city. Many Byzantines escaped and moved to Italy in exile; others remained and were allowed to have their own patriarch, George Scholarius. The period known to Greeks as the *Tourkokratia*, or Turkish domination, had begun.

Part 2

THE LEGACY

11

Byzantium and Orthodox
life and spirituality

The fall of Constantinople and the dispersal of many members of the Byzantine elite, followed by nearly five centuries of Ottoman rule in the central Byzantine territories, held back further attempts at healing the breach between east and west. But Byzantine Christianity survived and its legacy is continued in Orthodox churches today.

The members of these churches account for several hundred millions worldwide and are not confined to the countries of eastern Europe. Nor is Orthodoxy limited to the versions associated with Greece and Russia. There are other Orthodox churches all over the Balkans, in the Middle East and in many western countries too (see Chapter 14); the USA and Australia have large Orthodox communities. The term 'eastern Christianity' – distinct from the Roman Catholic and Protestant traditions – is often used as a general description, though it obscures the existence of Orthodox believers in other parts of the world. Some of the eastern churches, such as the Syrian Orthodox, the Copts, Georgians and Armenians, differ considerably from the Greek and Russian Orthodox, on whom I concentrate here, and there are in addition large numbers of Uniates, or Greek Catholics, who follow eastern rites but acknowledge the primacy of Rome (see Chapter 14).

As explained in Chapter 1, the term 'orthodox', without the initial capital, means only that the adherents claim to have the correct form of religion, just as the term 'catholic', already used in Latin in the time of Constantine, derives from the Greek and means 'universal', with no connection to the term 'Catholic' as used today. Both terms are claims rather than descriptions. Most Christians would indeed claim that they belong to the Church universal, but this is an aspiration rather than a realized fact.

The formation of doctrine will be discussed in Chapter 13. But religion is much more than an intellectual system or a body of beliefs; it is also about behaviour, practice and habits, and the influence of Byzantine Christianity is clear in the main aspects of Orthodox life and practice today.

Habits of worship and practical religion

Orthodox, Roman Catholic and Protestant Christians agree that Jesus was the Son of God and believe in the Trinity consisting of God the Father, God the Son and God the Holy Spirit. Jesus' mother Mary is believed to have been a virgin when he was conceived. These beliefs are expressed in regular worship and a structured annual round of Christian feasts or festivals – Advent, when the birth of Jesus is expected, Christmas, the season of his nativity or birth, Lent, the preparation for Easter, Easter, when he was crucified and resurrected, the Ascension, when he is believed to have gone up into heaven, and Pentecost, when the Holy Spirit was sent to the world (sometimes described as the birth of the Church). However, Orthodox Christian practice is set apart in many ways from that of the Roman Catholic and Protestant west, and very often these differences stem from its Byzantine heritage.

As in the west, the Orthodox churches have priests and bishops, but unlike in the Roman Catholic Church, priests can be married and have families, although bishops must be monastic and celibate. An order of female deaconesses existed during the Byzantine period, mainly ministering to other women, but women could not be ordained as priests. Apart from expressions of female lay piety, of which we hear a good deal in saints' lives and which is also demonstrated in inscriptions in churches and on religious objects, the main formal religious role open to them was to become nuns, and many did. Similarly the priesthood is closed to women in Orthodox churches today but there are many nuns. In mixed monasteries the men's and women's sections operate separately but the nuns need a male priest to preside at the Eucharist (known as the Divine Liturgy). Some monasteries dating back to the Byzantine period, such as those on Mount Athos and that of Saint Sabas near Jerusalem, do not allow women even as visitors, or strictly limit their access, as at Stavrovouni in Cyprus.

Orthodox Christians take a high view of the Church and the sacraments in which they believe God is revealed. The Eucharist, baptism and anointing with holy oil, confession, Christian marriage, the anointing of the sick and the three orders of priesthood – deacons, priests and bishops – are all central. They will seem familiar at first to western Christians, but differences of practice began early: Byzantines did not just continue to recite the Creed without the *Filioque*, but also mixed the (ordinary) bread with the wine and the wine with hot water. Elaborate hymns and music were a key feature of Byzantine liturgy, and many prayer books survive with appropriate hymns for different stages in the church calendar. But in most Orthodox churches the singing – except in female monasteries – is only male, and while organs were known in Byzantium they were not used in churches. 'Byzantine' church music today continues this tradition but also draws on other musical influences from the Ottoman era.

Many other features also have Byzantine origins. Mary, known in Greek since the Council of Ephesus as the *Theotokos* ('Bearer of God'), and referred to by Byzantines and Orthodox alike as the Mother of God (rather than as the Virgin, as in the west), is particularly venerated, with church feasts, shrines and churches. Her chief feast is the Feast of the Dormition on 15 August, commemorating the day on which her body was miraculously taken up to heaven. This is often depicted on icons, with Mary on her bier and Christ taking up her soul. A vast array of saints were venerated by Christians in Byzantium and that also continues in the Orthodox world; many saints are local, with their own annual feast days, and in Byzantium these festivals were often the occasion for markets and fairs. Many Orthodox Christians venerate special saints and keep icons of them at home, a practice also well known in Byzantium.

Worshippers in Orthodox churches kiss and bow down in front of icons, often in a particular order (see Chapter 12). Most also stand during worship and cross themselves in a different way from in the west, and there is less direct participation in the service by the congregation than in many western churches. The liturgical Greek often still in use even in the diaspora derives from the Byzantine period and is not the form of Greek spoken today. Orthodox churches are filled with icons of varying sizes and types rather than the religious statues that were a critical issue in the Protestant Reformation. Nor indeed has the Orthodox Church had a Reformation, and while there was an Orthodox Enlightenment, it took a different form from the Enlightenment in the west (see Chapter 14).

Social expressions of Orthodox life

Visiting shrines and places connected with particular saints was a major feature of Byzantine Christianity. In the earlier period, pilgrimage to the Holy Land represented an ambition for many Christians, and numerous accounts of such journeys have survived, in addition to the souvenirs that pilgrims brought home with them. Orthodox Christians visit holy places to pray and in the hope of blessings, and the invocation of particular saints is a fundamental part of their religious life; it is also an integral part of the calendar of church services celebrated through the year.

Almsgiving and the care of the poor and the sick were basic aspects of early Christianity. In Byzantium many monasteries also carried out these functions, and emperors and rich people endowed hospitals, old people's hospices and orphanages; bishops often controlled substantial resources and were expected to care for the poor and provide food in times of famine.

Byzantine practices continue to affect the daily life of Orthodox Christians. One of these is fasting on Wednesdays and Fridays, certain feast days and especially in Lent (meaning in its strictest form, abstention from meat, fish, dairy products, olive oil and wine), which has been practised since Byzantine times. Even if the rules are not always observed, they also illustrate the important influence of the liturgical calendar on the lives of Orthodox Christians. Divorce and up to three marriages are permitted, though not welcomed (the Emperor Leo VI's fourth marriage caused a serious crisis between emperor and Church – see Chapter 7). Regulations about whom one can marry also derive from the strict rules laid down by the Byzantine Church, forbidding marriage between relatives and others related by marriage.

Spirituality

An emphasis on spirituality is a key feature in Orthodoxy. It is derived directly from the Greek Fathers, including the Cappadocians – Basil, Gregory of Nyssa and Gregory of Nazianzus – and ascetic authorities such as Evagrius Ponticus and the Desert Fathers. Many extracts from their writings and sayings were gathered in the eighteenth century by Nicodemus, a monk of Mount Athos, and Macarius, metropolitan of Corinth, into a highly influential work known as the *Philokalia*, which ranks as one of the greatest influences on Orthodox Christianity. The *Philokalia* drew on the teachings of the Desert Fathers and emphasized constant prayer and contemplation as the means of access to God (also a fundamental feature of the hesychasm taught by Gregory Palamas in the fourteenth century – see Chapter 10).

The tradition represented in the *Philokalia* also emphasized the role of repentance in the life of the Orthodox Christian, and many icons represent the Last Judgement. Speculation about the afterlife was a prominent feature in Byzantine Christianity. But in the Orthodox Church, as in Byzantium, Christians also look to the possibility of *theosis*, or deification, meaning union with God, and are much less likely to dwell on Christ's suffering than was characteristic of the medieval west. In Orthodox churches, as in Byzantine ones, the worshipper is likely to see an image of the Theotokos in the apse, with Christ the Pantokrator, or 'Ruler of all', in the dome above.

The Scriptures and the Fathers

A major feature of Byzantine Christianity was the emphasis it laid on the authority of the Scriptures and the writings of the Greek Fathers. The same is true of Orthodoxy today, and one is also likely to find frescoes, mosaics or icons depicting the major Greek Fathers in any Orthodox church. The complaint was often made in Byzantium that the Latins relied on logic, and especially on syllogistic reasoning, whereas for Byzantines a reliance on early authorities was paramount. This contrast is not entirely fair; the Byzantines themselves deployed Aristotelian logic and syllogisms from an early date and continued to do so. But their reliance on authority is reflected in the conservatism in religious attitudes characteristic of the contemporary Orthodox world. If the primary test of orthodoxy is whether or not a given doctrine or practice can be shown to have been approved by reference to Scripture or the Fathers, change is likely to be represented as innovation and therefore rejected. A high view of the Church can also lead to a refusal to admit ecumenism on any terms or even to the denial of the term 'church' to other Christian groups (see Chapter 15).

Varieties of belief

In Byzantine Christianity a complex mesh of popular but widespread beliefs and practices existed alongside what one might term official doctrine and practice, ranging from magic and what might be called superstition to a lively belief in demons, ways of foretelling the future, expectations about the afterlife and a rich vein of apocryphal stories and legends about the saints. Striking similarities can be seen between Byzantine and contemporary practice in innumerable festivals, local traditions and beliefs, and many of these traditions, however difficult it may be to trace their origins and whatever their actual historic roots, retain a strong appeal and are faithfully maintained.

12

The setting of worship

The material legacy of Byzantine Christianity is evident in every country of eastern Europe and in many others with an Orthodox tradition. It can also be seen in major museums and collections all over the world. Exhibitions about Byzantium attract large numbers of visitors, even when the meaning and use of many of the items are unfamiliar. Byzantine art exerts a strong aesthetic pull, not least for its otherness and its association with gold and precious stones; this is perhaps the major contributor to the fascination with Byzantium still expressed today in so many novels and plays (see Chapter 15). Byzantine mosaics, like the frequently reproduced mosaics of Justinian and Theodora in Ravenna, seem at once familiar and foreign. The consciousness of Byzantium's eventual fall, combined with generations of adverse comparison with the classical world, has produced a general perception of decadence that itself fosters this overall fascination. This deep-seated western view of Byzantium is part of the latter's legacy, and contrasts sharply with the physical traces of Byzantium that matter for Orthodox Christians themselves and that have shaped the nature of Orthodox life and worship.

Byzantine Christianity and western European Christianity were both originally formed in a Mediterranean world in which the Roman empire was still united, and they share many basic features. The cult of saints and the veneration of Mary developed at about the same time in both east and west. Reliquaries, containers for the relics of saints (see below), can be found as much in Roman Catholic churches as Orthodox ones, though the former are likely to be adorned with statues rather than icons. But the display of newly painted or reproduced icons in some Anglican churches is a recent development arising from a growing interest in the worship of the eastern Church; popular icons in this category that are often reproduced include two famous Russian examples, the twelfth-century Virgin of Vladimir, originally from Kiev and now in Moscow, and the fifteenth-century icon painted by Andrei Rublev of Abraham being visited by the three angels, taken to symbolize the Trinity.

Church buildings

Countless churches still survive from the Byzantine period, from tiny village churches and private chapels to the vastness of Hagia Sophia in Istanbul. The Greek island of Naxos is not alone in allegedly having 365 churches, though many of them are small and were originally chapels on family land, used on feast days or for family commemorations of the dead. The remains of basilicas from the early Byzantine period can be seen all round the Mediterranean. They typically had apses marked off from the nave by low marble barriers. Some basilicas were very large showpiece churches capable of holding big congregations, others were much more modest. But there was no simple and straightforward development. Later Byzantine churches were typically domed, again with a huge variation in size, complexity and material, from the massive Hagia Sophia down to very modest constructions in local brick.

In other parts of the former empire, and after 1453, many local variations appeared but were clearly linked to Byzantine models through domes, plans and especially interior decoration. The icon-screen (iconostasis) in front of the sanctuary, with principal icons displayed on it, is a very familiar feature in Orthodox churches, again directly derived from Byzantium. Much variation is possible, but all Orthodox churches are likely to have mosaic or fresco cycles of scenes from the lives of Christ and the *Theotokos*, depictions of major and local saints and the most important Church Fathers, and typically the Virgin and child in the apse and Christ Pantokrator in the dome.

Icons

Icons are the most obvious markers of Orthodox worship, and are found in large numbers in every church and in many homes. The eleventh-century Empress Zoe is said to have been devoted to icons that she would hold and kiss, and many Orthodox homes today have an icon corner with a collection of favourites. Reproduction icons of every size and quality are on sale in souvenir shops and on stalls, and often hang above the windscreen in cars.

As mentioned in Chapter 5, it is important to note that the term 'icon' was not limited in Byzantium to painted panels, the most familiar type of icon known today. The Greek word *eikon* simply means 'image', and could be applied also to depictions of the saints, Christ or Mary in other media, whether on mosaics and frescoes or on small reliefs, book covers, rings and belts or indeed woven in fabric and worn on clothes. Nevertheless the painted panel is what most people identify as an icon. On entering an Orthodox church, worshippers 'greet' the icons with a kiss and a bow, usually in a certain order of importance, starting with the feast icon at the entrance of the church and going on to the major icons on the iconostasis. Some icons are believed to have miraculous powers of healing, protection or intervention, as in Byzantium. They are often carried in procession, yet another Byzantine feature. The painful arguments of the iconoclast period resulted in the understanding that the icon itself was venerated but not worshipped and that the veneration was given to the holy person depicted in it, not to the material object itself, but these are fine distinctions, and some icons receive special degrees of veneration. These include those images believed to be 'not made with human hands' – that is, miraculously produced – and the several icons of Mary believed to have been painted by Saint Luke or to have miraculous powers. There are several sixth- or seventh-century images of Mary in Rome, which was unaffected by Byzantine iconoclastic destruction. Byzantine Constantinople placed special faith in its icon of Mary with the child on her lap, known as the Hodegetria ('she who points the way'), and while the original has not survived, there are countless other examples of this iconography in both eastern and western medieval art. Famous images, especially of Christ or Mary, are still believed to have powers of healing and the ability to perform miracles.

Relics

The veneration of saints in Byzantium embraced not only the proliferation of images, the regular reading of extracts from the lives of the saints on feast days and visits and pilgrimages to shrines and places associated with individual saints or groups of saints, but also the preservation and veneration of their relics – bones, fragments of their bodies, garments or whole bodies believed to have been miraculously preserved. The collection and 'finding' of such relics began early, in the fourth century, and was closely associated with the cult of Christians martyred or believed to have been martyred in the Roman persecutions. Ambitious bishops acquired relics for their new churches or had them 'translated', or moved, from other places, and thus gained great popular kudos. Whether they were of local saints or of major figures, the relics of saints were believed to confer protection and to be very efficacious in getting prayers answered. Such relics were buried beneath the altar in churches, or encased in reliquaries, boxes or holders, often made of gold or silver and adorned with precious stones, or in small lockets that could be worn by pious individuals. Every museum with a Byzantine collection will have numerous examples, both private and ecclesiastical, as also of the tokens brought back by pilgrims (see below). By the middle and late Byzantine periods, such reliquaries were ubiquitous and ranged from simple devotional objects to highly elaborate examples of refined workmanship. A few wealthy people wore them on their persons in lockets and pendants.

The cult of relics developed alongside that of icons. Constantinople claimed the robe and the girdle of the Virgin, as well as numerous objects associated with the crucifixion of Christ – the nails, the lance that pierced his side and the crown of thorns he was forced to wear. Passion relics were greatly sought after. The supposed fragments of the cross on which Christ was crucified were, erroneously, believed to derive from a discovery made by Helena, the mother of

Constantine, during the excavation for the church of the Holy Sepulchre in Jerusalem. They too found their way to the west as well as to the lands under Byzantine influence, and can be found, or are claimed to exist, in western as well as eastern churches. An early church in Rome, Santa Croce in Gerusalemme, commemorates Helena's discovery and claims to contain Passion relics from Jerusalem. When the Crusaders gained control of Jerusalem and the Christian holy places, they too commissioned mosaics and frescoes on the Byzantine model, but with western adaptations. In later periods countless medieval and Renaissance artists in Italy and elsewhere decorated churches with their versions not only of the Passion of Christ and the Gospel narratives themselves but also of the legendary finding of the cross by Helena.

Religious objects

Museums and collections are also full of objects illustrating the attachment of Byzantine Christians to personal possessions with religious themes; there must be many thousands of these in existence. They range from amulets, charms and tokens with religious figures or wording to the souvenirs brought back from pilgrimages and holy places. Amulets connected with childbirth and women's health are particularly common. Small clay lamps with Christian symbols or clay tokens with portraits of the saint or with abbreviations of prayers, or glass bottles containing oil, earth or water, were all manufactured at popular shrines and brought back in huge numbers by pilgrims and visitors. Pilgrimage itself was big business. The shrine of Thecla in southern Turkey, much visited in the early Byzantine period, produced many hundreds, or even thousands, of pilgrim souvenirs, and these made their way all over the Mediterranean; the same development took place at other important shrines, some of which came to prominence later in the Byzantine period, and is a phenomenon well attested at medieval shrines in Europe. These pilgrim objects were known as 'blessings' and were believed to have special capacities for ensuring the health and welfare of their owners. They are not usually elite or expensive items, and they are evidence of a wide-spread popular religiosity.

Some Byzantines were rich enough to possess personal items such as earrings, rings, belts or various kinds of pendants, made of gold or silver and with inlay and enamel, with religious images and wording on them. Precious examples were also given as diplomatic gifts but many are much more modest. Some Byzantines wore miniature Gospel books or texts round their necks and many wore crosses with religious figures or inscriptions. Again, many examples can be found in museum collections and have their counterparts today; 'Byzantine' jewellery is also a popular item in museum shops. A small number of the richest and most aristocratic among Byzantine Christians might own decorated book covers enclosing prayer books or other religious texts in manuscript form (unfortunately for Byzantium, the fall of Constantinople happened just as the printing press was invented). Most such book covers now to be found in collections, and especially Gospel book covers, were commissioned for use in churches and monasteries, and many were ornamented with religious figures or scenes.

Most collections also contain examples of liturgical objects used during Byzantine church services and in Orthodox churches today, especially communion vessels and spoons, often made of silver. The vestments worn by Orthodox priests and bishops – and in many Catholic churches too – derive ultimately from garments worn in the early centuries of Christianity, although the typical head-wear developed later, and practice varies in the different eastern churches.

13

Discipline and control

Christianity in Byzantium was not merely a matter of lay and popular piety. It was also characterized by the efforts of the Church and its leaders to lay down rules for belief and conduct and to control the lives of the faithful. Indeed, there were many variations of belief and practice among Byzantine Christians of every period, as the repeated efforts to assert control tell us. Furthermore, on the whole we hear little from ordinary people themselves. Saints' lives contain many details apparently about ordinary life, but as they were written to praise their subject, the information in them always has to be read with caution. All the same, it is clear that Byzantine Christians had to live within a system that set out to be highly regulated and which encompassed their beliefs and their daily lives. This is the case even though the 'system' itself was often challenged, while differences in belief and practice always existed, and most people – as also today – probably did not appreciate the finer points of theology. Not all religions have such regulatory characteristics, though many do. But the model of Christianity bequeathed by Byzantium was that of an all-encompassing system and a Church that claimed a high degree of authority over its members.

Doctrinal systems

Byzantine Christians took doctrine seriously. The impetus behind the Council of Nicaea summoned by the Emperor Constantine in 325 was to achieve agreement across the empire about matters of Christian doctrine and practice. The divisions that he had found between Christians in different parts of the empire and even within individual communities went back to the early Christian period, long before Constantine's day. Nor, as we have seen, did they end with the Council of Nicaea. It is no exaggeration to say that argument and division were characteristic of the entire history of Byzantine Christianity.

'Theology' refers to the study and understanding of God, which for the Byzantines referred to the technical aspects of the relation of the Father, the Son and the Holy Spirit, the status of Mary and the saints and to many issues of detailed interpretation. The Scriptures, the Fathers (see Chapter 3) and the councils constituted the basis of Byzantine theology, and constant appeal was made to their authority. But the Scriptures needed interpretation, the Fathers did not always agree, and councils took place only because there was division. The Fathers, and later Byzantine theologians after them, composed vast quantities of treatises, letters, homilies, commentaries and other works, with the aim of producing a comprehensive system of correct doctrine, and the eastern churches today have inherited both the same emphasis on past authority, and its implied conservatism. Though it fails to do justice to their own theological sophistication and deployment of logic, there is something in the view that the Byzantines relied especially on the concept of tradition and on citing authorities. This makes for an inherently conservative approach among modern Orthodox churches.

Heresy

Alongside an emphasis on forming a comprehensive theo-logical system goes the identification and condemnation of rival formulations. Both were evident in all periods of Byzantine Christianity and have left a powerful legacy, even to the extent that non-Orthodox churches are sometimes regarded as heretical. Some eastern Orthodox therefore reject the concept of ecumenism on the grounds that their own Church is the only true Church.

In the late fourth century and again in the fifth, imperial laws proscribed heresy, setting an example followed by later emperors. But emperors could also fall into heresy: at the end of his life the sixth-century Emperor Justinian was persuaded by views others considered heretical, and some seventh- and eighth-century emperors imposed doctrines that were later condemned. We have seen already how these tendencies con-tinued throughout the Byzantine period. But the idea that there must be one officially approved version of Christian doctrine was fundamental to Byzantine Christianity, with the corollary that others were wrong. Doctrinal argument did not stop, but centuries of repeated doctrinal statements and formulations only intensified the conviction held by all that there could not be more than one system of correct belief.

Such a conviction has made for difficulty in the mod-ern period in relations with other churches. The high view of the Church held by most Orthodox can easily slide into rigorism, even when the official church hierarchies do not take such a line. Clearly there are many differences between

Orthodox communities across the world and a variety of attitudes. However, Orthodox rigorists, including some elements within the Russian and Greek Orthodox churches, and in the Russian Church Outside Russia, appeal to a supposedly unbroken tradition and a purist ideal. They have included the Old Believers in Russia and the 'old calendrists' who adhere on principle to the Julian calendar rather than the New Calendar adopted by the Greek Orthodox Church and the patriarchate of Constantinople in the twentieth century (some other eastern churches also retain the Julian calendar). Rigorist attitudes often go with anti-westernism and anti-modernism, and are vehemently opposed to liberalism and relativism.

Such attitudes can also be seen to some extent as a Byzantine legacy. In Byzantium the term 'heretic' was commonly used, as we have seen, and its application was very elastic. The fact that orthodoxy was held to rest in an unspecified combination of the Scriptures, the writings of the Fathers and decisions of the councils meant that it remained possible to argue about what it actually was. This tendency to engage in internal argument and the splits between groups are also legacies from Byzantium.

Jews and Muslims

Hostile writing about Judaism began early in the Christian era as Christians sought to separate themselves and identify Judaism as something other, and to win over Christians who were perceived as being too sympathetic to Jewish practices. During the Byzantine period many writers followed earlier precedent and composed polemical works directed against Judaism, and with the advent of Islam in the seventh century onwards, similar arguments began to be made against Muslims. In this discourse, which was deeply embedded in Byzantine attitudes, both Jews and Muslims were often equated with heretics, and similar vocabulary applied to them. The effect of such an inheritance limited actual Byzantine engagement with Islam and made the increasing pressure on Byzantium from the Muslim Turks even harder to deal with. Some of these tensions continued to manifest themselves in later centuries. They pose deep questions for Orthodox churches about the conception of the Orthodox Church as universal, and about salvation – whether, or on what terms, persons outside the Church can still be saved.

Ecclesiastical law

The private lives and moral behaviour of Byzantine Christians were also closely regulated. Church councils ruled from an early date on such matters as well as on church organization and belief, and from the late sixth century onwards these regulations were gradually collected and systematized into a body of canon law that existed alongside the legal system of the empire. The council of 692 held in Constantinople was convened specifically to issue canons, since neither of the previous two councils had done so. The Byzantine law codes of the eighth century and later brought the legal system inherited from the late Roman empire more and more into line with Christian principles. The Emperor Constantine had set a precedent by granting bishops legal authority, and in later centuries many people took their cases to ecclesiastical courts, especially in family matters.

Both the moral regulation, conveyed by many different means including spiritual advice and sermons in church, and the weight given to canon law and ecclesiastical juris-diction have survived in Orthodox churches. Central issues affecting Orthodox Christians include rulings on mar-riage and divorce, fasting and penitence and the keeping of church feasts and the church calendar, all of them deriving from Byzantine precedent. It is no accident that the same Nicodemus of Mount Athos who produced the *Philokalia* in the eighteenth century (see Chapter 11) also produced a highly influential manual of canon law.

Oikonomia

Despite these efforts to create an all-encompassing and uni-versal religious system expressive of the 'divine economy' (*oikonomia*, God's providential direction of the world), there was no authority in Byzantine Christianity to compare with the Roman Catholic *magisterium*. Strictness (*akribeia*), or allegiance to the letter of the law, could be tempered by invoking the concept of *oikonomia* in a different sense, indi-cating a resort to discretion in imitation of God's mercy. The word 'economy' means in general 'management' or 'steward-ship', and could also be applied to what we call economics, as well as to the running of a monastery. In the present sense the application of *oikonomia* in individual cases was held to be a recognition of humankind's fallen condition and need for the grace and mercy of God, and could be invoked to justify a softening of the severe punishments otherwise laid down. Even though in Byzantium, as we have seen, many clerics and others did suffer severe ecclesiastical sanctions, the principle of *oikonomia* represents a characteristic view in Byzantine and Orthodox Christianity of the merciful nature of God and the workings of divine grace.

14

Orthodox churches and others

The split with Rome

The gradual separation of the Roman and Byzantine churches, and of Byzantine Christianity and churches further east, lies behind the division between eastern and western churches today. As we have seen, the split between Byzantium and the Church of Rome had a far longer and more complex history than is suggested by references to a 'Great Schism' in 1054. The western addition of the *Filioque* to the Creed was a major stumbling block and gave rise to ever-increasing amounts of theological argument. But the most fundamental issue was the western claim to Roman primacy, especially as it developed later in the medieval period. Acceptance of the seniority of the Roman patriarchate was one thing; accepting the overall authority of the pope was another.

When Constantinople finally fell in 1453, the act of union agreed in Florence in 1438 was technically in force but Byzantine Christians were deeply divided. But everything changed with the imposition of Ottoman rule.

Orthodox Christians in the Ottoman empire

In many of the former territories of Byzantium, Orthodox Christianity continued to exist in the new context of the

Ottoman empire, and the Byzantine legacy continued to be felt. However, the period of Ottoman rule left deep traces. Not all the former empire fell within Ottoman territories. Byzantium exerted a direct influence on the Christianity of Kievan Rus', and the Byzantine legacy later passed to Moscow; the claim was made that Russia was the 'third Rome' (Rome itself being regarded as heretical and Constantinople, the 'new Rome', being under Muslim rule), and a patriarchate was established in 1589. As in Bulgaria, Russian Orthodoxy developed in the vernacular, and at times its relations with post-Byzantine Greek Orthodoxy were a source of tension.

In the Ottoman empire the Church was tolerated by Mehmet II and his successors, and Gennadius Scholarius was appointed patriarch by the sultan within a year of the conquest. But the intellectual ties with early Renaissance Italy that had characterized the last century of Byzantine rule were now closed off. There was no longer a Christian emperor, and the theoretical balance in Byzantium – however imperfect – between emperor and patriarch, state and Church, was broken. The Church took on the uncontested leadership of the Christian population but was also subject to the Ottoman sultan. The patriarch now functioned as an intermediary, receiving privileges, including the right to collect taxes, but in return acquiring duties to the Ottoman state and paying an annual tribute and other financial dues. Patriarchs often found themselves in financial difficulties, and when their tax-raising efforts were unsuccessful they had to turn for support to wealthy laypersons, who thus acquired an influence over them, or to the sultans. This was an unenviable position, and while making the patriarch the beneficiary of lands and property owned by monasteries and episcopal sees, it placed him in the invidious role of tax collector.

Hagia Sophia was in use as a mosque and the patriarch had to use a lesser church. Conversion to Islam was a way of freeing individuals from the burdens of the special taxes required of non-Muslims, and this reduced the size of the Christian population. Churches were in danger of being turned into mosques, and the patriarchate effectively changed hands for money, leading to a rapid turnover. Even so, some notable patriarchs were able to use their position to make alliances and to respond to the changing political and religious situation outside. At the end of the sixteenth century the patriarch Jeremias II visited Poland and Muscovy, and his visit resulted in the formation of the patriarchate in Moscow. This gradual extension of the reach of the patriarchate in Constantinople laid the foundations for the broader influence claimed by the ecumenical patriarchate today.

Pressures from Rome

Nothing, however, contributed to a lessening of hostility to the Church of Rome. The reform of the Julian calendar under Pope Gregory XIII was greeted with suspicion as a western innovation. Jesuit missionary activity within the Ottoman empire, their school in Constantinople and their attempts to exercise influence over the patriarchate added to the ill-feeling. A further threat came from the efforts of Rome to win over eastern Christians by encouraging them to acknowledge the primacy of Rome while maintaining their own liturgical traditions; a Greek college was founded in Rome in 1577 with this as its aim. These are the eastern

Catholics, sometimes called Uniates, who now exist in large numbers alongside Orthodox Christians in many countries and in the worldwide diaspora. They include the Ukrainian Greek Catholics, whose history goes back to the late sixteenth century and who were suppressed under communist rule, and the Maronites and Chaldaeans in the Middle East, where they contribute to a highly complex and often fragmented religious scenario. The patriarchate of Antioch in Syria was one of the five historic patriarchates of the early Church, but these later developments have led to the existence of a plurality of patriarchs of Antioch from different churches, including Greek Orthodox, Syrian Orthodox and three eastern Catholic churches.

Relations with Protestants

There were Orthodox contacts with Lutherans at Tübingen and correspondence between them following the Augsburg Confession of 1530. In the seventeenth century a few Greek scholars and churchmen studied at Balliol College, Oxford, among them Metrophanes Kritopoulos, who was also sent by the patriarch to churches and universities in Germany and Switzerland. His *Confession* of 1625 was addressed to the Lutherans of Helmstadt and he also addressed questions to the Calvinists in Geneva. Aware of the need for education, the patriarchate established a Greek college in Oxford at the end of the seventeenth century, and money was raised and building begun for a Greek church in London. However, this mutual interest soon foundered when differences emerged between the Anglicans and the Orthodox and the church was sold. The Greek college was also short-lived. Nevertheless the Orthodox shared with the Protestants a common hostility to Rome, and some, especially the patriarch Cyril Loukaris (patriarch with two interruptions from 1620 to 1638), were sympathetic to Protestant views. Loukaris was in contact with the Archbishop of Canterbury and through him with King James I; he had been educated in Padua and travelled to Vilna and Lvov, where he saw Roman proselytizing and religious divisions at first hand. His *Confession*, published in Greek in Geneva in 1631, had a distinctly Calvinist tone but aroused Orthodox opposition and gave the Turkish authorities an opportunity; he was executed in 1638 and his *Confession* condemned.

Knowledge of Orthodoxy grew as accounts of the Greek Church, Mount Athos and Constantinople reached England. In 1716 the non-jurors, Anglicans unwilling to sign the oath of allegiance to William and Mary, made overtures to the Orthodox and set out many points of similarity, though also some differences. But their overtures were rejected, and while they received a more sympathetic response from Peter the Great of Russia, the latter's death put an end to such contacts. If there had ever been realistic hopes of closer relations between the Greek Church and Protestants, their differences had also been revealed. There has been contemporary dialogue between Anglicans and Orthodox since the 1970s; it focuses on common ground but proceeds at a very slow pace.

An Orthodox Enlightenment?

The New Testament was translated into modern Greek in 1703, and in the eighteenth century, influences from the west had an impact in certain parts of the Orthodox world. Evgenios Voulgaris of Corfu (1716–1806) studied in

Padua and taught in Ioannina in northern Greece. He was appointed by the then patriarch to head a new 'Academy' on Mount Athos and later the patriarchal school in Constantinople. But the new science and new philosophy aroused objections, and Voulgaris moved to Russia, ruled at the time by Catherine the Great. Voulgaris's younger contemporary, Nikiphoros Theotokis (1731–1800), also studied in Padua and taught in Constantinople, but encountered opposition and moved to Jassy in Moldavia before he too left for Russia. Yet another and more militant advocate of western European secular thought to the Orthodox world was Iosipos Moisiodax (1725–1800). But the French Revolution caused Orthodox suspicion to intensify into outright opposition to secularism and to the influence of Voltaire. Not all sympathy for western philosophy and science was quenched, but the events in France provoked direct and hostile responses.

Orthodoxy and national churches

During the nineteenth century the patriarchate in Constantinople found itself affected by the political ramifications of Ottoman decline. A series of independence movements began within the empire, with Serbian uprisings from 1804 onwards and the Greek war of independence and the establishment of the modern Greek state in 1832. These developments presented immediate dilemmas and had major consequences for the Church, as, despite objections to what is called 'ethnophyletism', national churches progressively gained autonomy and then autocephaly and the appointment of a patriarch. Serbia was granted autonomy in 1831 and autocephaly after the Treaty of Berlin in 1878. Local

churches in Yugoslavia were unified under a single patriarch of Serbia in 1924. A similar trajectory was followed
in Romania, with autocephaly in 1885 and a patriarchate in
1925. In Bulgaria an exarchate was agreed by the Ottoman
state in 1870 but opposed by the patriarchate as schismatic;
the schism was finally lifted only in 1945 when autocephaly was also recognized. In Greece the legacy of Byzantium,
and especially of its Orthodoxy, reasserted itself in the nineteenth century despite the classicizing ideals of the newly
independent Greek state, and found political expression
in the 'Great Idea', the hoped-for recovery of Constantinople.
The latter ended in tragic failure in Asia Minor in 1922, followed by the exchange of populations in 1923 that brought
the forcible relocation to Greece of large numbers of
Orthodox Christians hitherto living in Turkey.

The ecumenical patriarchate thus found itself under
pressure even before the major changes that led to the foundation of the Turkish republic in 1923. Today the patriarchate is still based in Istanbul, but claims a wide influence based
on its seniority as a consequence of its history. In practice,
however, it cannot insist on this against determined opposition from other Orthodox churches, as was evident at the
Great and Holy Council held on Crete in 2016 (see Chapter
15). It has close connections with Greece, whose Church
has autocephalous status under an archbishop, but its relation to the modern Greek state remains complex, while its
position in an increasingly Islamic Turkey seems even more
precarious than before.

The Russian Revolution led to a widespread dispersal
of Russian Orthodox and to the establishment of ROCOR
(the Russian Orthodox Church Outside Russia), which sep-
arated from Moscow in 1927. Russian émigrés in Paris and

elsewhere were at the forefront of a rediscovery of the patristic heritage of spirituality. As for ROCOR, it is only one of numerous churches in the diaspora, where Orthodoxy remains highly fragmented, with liturgical differences adding to its complexity; efforts were made by the ecumenical patriarchate to reduce this variety in the Council of 2016 but failed. Communist rule put the Orthodox churches under extreme strain; opinions about the role played by the Orthodox Church in the Soviet Union differed sharply, and indeed led to schism. But the revival of the Moscow patriarchate since the thousand-year anniversary of the baptism of Vladimir in 1988, and especially since 1991 and under Vladimir Putin, has brought a strong reassertion of its influence inside and outside Russia. ROCOR signed an act of communion with Moscow in 2007.

In all these churches, however diverse, the Byzantine legacy remains a given in terms of practice, shared history, and spirituality. The mystical tradition inherited from Byzantium is especially evident in Russian Orthodoxy. Many of the characteristics of Byzantine Christianity can also still be observed in what might be termed 'grassroots' Orthodoxy (see Chapter 11). In some countries, especially under communism, popular traditions with very mixed origins have aided the survival of Orthodox feeling and practice. But certain fundamentals are common to all the different churches that now make up the Orthodox world and Orthodoxy worldwide. They are ties of sentiment and outlook and include the emphasis laid on the traditions of the Fathers and the canons, the exclusion of women from the priesthood and a high view of the Church and the liturgy and its ancient roots that brings particular difficulties in ecumenical relations with non-Orthodox churches, and still more with other faiths.

15

Perspectives today

The direct legacy of later Byzantine Christianity

The direct legacy of later Byzantine Christianity can be clearly seen both within the Orthodox world and much more widely. It has an impact on our own culture, understanding of history and aesthetic tastes, as well as on religions and religious practice worldwide. With the collapse of the Soviet Union and the subsequent developments in Russia, eastern Europe and the Middle East, it also has an impact on contemporary world politics. In modern Turkey the secular agenda of the Turkish republic left no place for the Byzantine religious legacy, and despite a recent upturn in academic interest in Byzantine religious monuments, the increasingly Islamic nature of the state in recent years has meant, for instance, that frescoes in the late Byzantine church of Hagia Sophia in Trabzon (late medieval Trebizond) have been covered in connection with the building's return to use as a mosque. A call for similar action in the case of Hagia Sophia in Istanbul has not so far been implemented. At the same time Syrian Orthodox Christians in eastern Turkey are again under pressure. Many of the Christian communities in the Middle East that have inherited the Byzantine legacy are also under serious threat from the turmoil in Iraq and Syria. It is imperative to understand the religious as well as the political implications of the rise of Putin's Russia. In the

Balkans, Serbia and Bulgaria, as well as Greece, are strongly Orthodox, and elsewhere in the Balkans the Byzantine legacy is strongly felt and exerted, with Orthodox churches competing for space and influence with Islam and with other Christian denominations.

The serious academic study of Byzantium began only in the late nineteenth century and was led by art historians. In comparison with the study and knowledge of classical antiquity it remains a poor relation. Yet understanding the nature of the Byzantine religious legacy and why it matters has never been more important.

This final chapter will survey some of the features of that legacy that are very much alive today. They range from the external and the cultural to fundamental features of practice and emphasis deriving from Byzantine Christianity that contrast with Roman Catholic and Protestant Christianity.

Music, art and literature

Byzantine worship was a sensory experience, and among the influences of Byzantine Christianity in contemporary culture outside the Orthodox sphere the most obvious is its aesthetic appeal in the fields of music, poetry and drama, and of course art and architecture.

Unaccompanied chanting and singing are features of Orthodox services, and the complex liturgical tradition and elaborate hymnography of Byzantine Christianity are still reflected in contemporary practice. Byzantine music and chant, the singing of Russian male choirs and performances of such works as Rachmaninov's *Vespers* of 1915 – deriving from the All-Night Vigil of the Russian Orthodox

Church – all have a wide general appeal. So too does the later music of the Estonian composer Arvo Pärt, a convert from Lutheranism to Russian Orthodoxy.

Many works by the English composer John Tavener (d. 2013) owe their inspiration to the Byzantine tradition. Tavener was a convert to Orthodoxy and his music subsequently became increasingly based on his study of the Byzantine Christian legacy. Tavener described his compositions as icons in sound, and works such as *The Protecting Veil* and *Song for Athene*, performed at the funeral of Princess Diana in 1997, powerfully evoke the distinctive legacy of Byzantium.

Even better known is the literary impact of Byzantine Christianity. W. B. Yeats's poem 'Sailing to Byzantium' (1926) may be the most famous and most often quoted example, but it is far from the only one (another can be found in the work of the Greek poet C. P. Cavafy). Yeats's lines

> such a form as Grecian goldsmiths make
> Of hammered gold and gold enamelling
> To keep a drowsy Emperor awake

represent a vision of mystery, luxury and immortality, and offer a powerful evocation of an exotic world that has shaped countless imaginative recreations of Byzantium.

The Empress Theodora has been a particularly powerful literary inspiration. In the famous mosaic in the church of San Vitale, Ravenna, she is shown leading a eucharistic procession; it is an image depicted in numerous books on Byzantium, and often on their covers. She is a frequent subject for novelists and playwrights, and was played by Sarah Bernhardt in Victorien Sardou's *Théodora* in nineteenth-century Paris. A hippodrome performer who became an empress, Theodora represents aspects of Byzantium that have had an enduring fascination, increased by Procopius's description of her lengthy toilettes and haughty manner and his titillating account of her performances before her marriage. But Theodora also demonstrates the legacy of Byzantine Christianity. She actively supported anti-Chalcedonian monks and clergy and involved herself closely in religious affairs. Accordingly she is remembered in the Syrian Orthodox tradition as a pious queen rather than an empress with a shady past.

The most obvious aesthetic influence of Byzantine Christianity is exerted through its art, especially icons, mosaics, frescoes, Gospel books, enamels, ivories and other precious objects (see Chapter 12). The frequency with which terms such as 'gold', 'treasure', 'glory', 'power' and 'spirituality' appear in the titles of recent exhibitions on Byzantium, as also in so many books on Byzantine art, is enough in itself to demonstrate the power of this appeal. A very high proportion of surviving Byzantine art is Christian art, and many examples are designed to convey complex doctrinal messages. Byzantine religious art needs explanation, and that may indeed be part of its very appeal.

Ecclesiology

The Byzantine Christian legacy is also vividly displayed in the contrast between the ecclesiology of the Orthodox churches and that of the Roman Church. This contrast was illustrated in 2016 in the Great and Holy Council held on the island of Crete, when the very fact that the eastern Christian model is one of conciliarity rather than authority enabled several national churches to refuse to participate.

Appeal is made in Orthodoxy to tradition and to the church canons (see Chapter 13), but as we have seen, tradition can be differently interpreted, and the canons do not provide a systematic and definitive source of church law. The Council of 2016 was declared a success but much of its success consisted in the considerable achievement shown in the holding of such a council at all, the first for centuries, and held only after decades of preparation.

Difficult issues in relation to ecumenism include recognition of other churches, which was another reason for opposition to the Council of 2016; still another is the staunch Orthodox opposition to the ordination of women (and to same-sex relations). While the anathemas proclaimed in 1054 have been officially lifted and discussions with the Roman Catholic Church have now taken a more fraternal tone, the conservative Orthodox stance deriving directly from the Byzantine Christian legacy still holds.

Church and state relations

The legacy of Byzantium can also be felt in the relations between Church and state in some Orthodox countries. According to Byzantine political philosophy the emperor was the vice-gerent of God, and later Byzantine emperors claimed an authoritative position in relation to the Church. There was no clear separation of powers: relations between Church and state were close and interconnected, while also leaving the possibility of the tensions and divisions described earlier. A particularly high doctrine of the Church was formulated in the last period of the Byzantine empire. In Greece, Russia, Bulgaria and elsewhere, the relation of the Church to the state is also close but can be difficult at times, albeit in different ways. And while the Orthodox Church today claims universality, it includes national churches that exist in tension with the overall influence of the ecumenical patriarch. In the post-communist world the Church is again being used for political ends, especially in Putin's Russia. Such manipulation also reaches to Moscow's influence in the diaspora. At the same time it must be said that the revival of Orthodoxy there and elsewhere in former communist countries has genuine popular roots among young as well as old, and is by no means only driven by the state.

Christians in the Middle East

Today Christians in the Middle East are increasingly threatened and the ancient roots of Christianity forgotten or denied. Despite this, many different kinds of Christianity can still be found, among which the Coptic Church in Egypt is one of the larger groupings.

The presence of Christianity in the Middle East derives directly from the spread of Christianity in the early centuries and the early Byzantine empire. Bishoprics were established early all over the eastern Mediterranean world, and three out of the five ancient patriarchates – Antioch, Jerusalem and Alexandria – were in the east. It was the divisions that arose after the Councils of Ephesus and Chalcedon (see Chapter 3) that eventually led to a more plural Christian organization and that are reflected in the wide variety among contemporary Christian communities across the region. In the early period the influence of Constantinople and Alexandria extended to Ethiopia and south-west Arabia (contemporary Yemen). The legacy of

Byzantine Christianity is also felt in Syria, Iraq, Iran and the Persian Gulf, and it made its mark directly on the Qur'anic message. When the Umayyad caliphate was established in the seventh century with its capital at Damascus, Christians remained the great majority among the population and the rulers relied on them in their administration. The long tradition of Christian writers in Syriac who engaged in dialogue with Islam also began in the Umayyad period. After the Arab conquests and during the early Islamic period a strong learned culture was maintained among Syriac-speaking Christians, and they played a central role in translating this culture – including Greek philosophy – and transmitting it to Baghdad. It is usually claimed that the Greek philosophical tradition passed directly into Arabic and was thus preserved, but translations from Greek into Syriac, already frequent in the fifth and sixth centuries, works in Syriac and the activity of Christian scholars were key to this cultural transfer.

Personal spirituality and religious life

A different legacy from Byzantium is that of personal spirituality, influenced by the patristic tradition of spiritual writing and its expression in the *Philokalia* (see Chapter 11). A major part of the Byzantine Christian legacy lies in the monastic tradition, still very strong in the eastern Church. The aspiration to live a hermit's life as a solitary is still the ambition of many Orthodox monks and nuns, and is regarded as a higher form of spiritual and physical practice than the communal monastic life. But lay piety has also been much influenced by this emphasis on personal spirituality, which also allows women a respected place.

The legacy of hesychasm, with its emphasis on the Jesus Prayer (see Chapter 10), remains strong within Orthodoxy and is also attractive to many non-Orthodox Christians. Mystical theology, including the symbolic understanding of the Church, is directly inherited from the early Greek Fathers and from Byzantine Christianity. So are the prayer of the heart and the emphasis on the possibility of *theosis* (divinization) for all, in contrast with the western and Augustinian tradition of original sin or emphasis on the salvation of the elect. Sin and repentance were certainly central themes in Byzantine Christianity, but the major Greek Fathers, Maximus Confessor, John of Damascus and Gregory Palamas, were much more powerful and direct influences than Augustine. Similarly, while the Passion of Christ was of course also a central issue in Byzantine theology, the forms of medieval piety familiar in the west have left far less trace.

A holistic view of creation and of men and women in the world

Orthodox Christians share with Byzantines a view of the world that sees God as involved in all aspects of creation, and does not separate matter and spirit. It follows that men and women are also fully part of this communion, a communion that should ideally also exist between the individual and God. The designation of churches and of the liturgy as representing heaven on earth is another way of expressing this sense of participation and involvement. In the same way the aim of the canons and other regulations that were part of Byzantine Christianity was to create a system for the whole of Christian life and experience. At its best it was an ideal that gave the individual a powerful sense of belonging and support.

Environmentalism

A distinctive feature of Orthodoxy today is the approach it takes towards issues of ecology and environmentalism. This may seem an unlikely example of the influence of Byzantine Christianity, yet it derives from the holistic view taken in Byzantium of divine and human matters and of the pervading influence of God in every aspect of the world. As was argued by the defenders of icons during the period of Byzantine iconoclasm, the natural world and the place of matter and material creation are regarded as integral to the whole. God's creation is therefore a gift to be approached eucharistically and sacramentally. The cosmos itself is a communion, and honouring the environment is a way of recognizing God. Such a view draws deeply on Byzantine writers, especially Maximus Confessor.

The Cyrillic alphabet and Slavonic Christianity

Finally, it was because of the Byzantine missions to the Slavs that the Slavonic alphabet now in use in modified form in Russian and other languages, including Bulgarian, Serbian and Macedonian, was created. The Cyrillic alphabet is named after the ninth-century Byzantine missionary Saint Cyril, although it seems to have developed somewhat later, and Byzantine support for the use of the vernacular was an important initiative that lies behind the emergence of a distinctive Slavonic Christianity.

Conclusion

The history of Byzantium is often ignored in favour of a narrative focused on western Europe. However, as many scholars now argue, neither the history of Europe nor that of the Mediterranean and the Middle East can be understood without it. Byzantine Christianity derives from the earliest period of Christian history. Much of what we take for granted in Christian thought and experience was formed in the eastern context rather than in the Latin west. From Byzantium, Christianity also spread further eastwards, even reaching China. In modern times, Orthodox diasporas have become established all over the world.

The inheritance of Byzantine Christianity has directly shaped the religious and in many ways also the political framework of a large group of countries in which Orthodoxy is the main form of Christian expression, and in the conditions of post-communist Europe its influence is rapidly growing. In such a situation there is a pressing need for better understanding, and this is even more necessary in view of the added complexity caused by the existence of large numbers of Uniates in Romania, the Ukraine, the Middle East and elsewhere. In such a situation it is all the more necessary to resist formulations according to which there is a single 'Orthodox civilization' to be contrasted with that of the west.

But the legacy of Byzantine Christianity reaches far beyond the Orthodox world. Many in the west are unfamiliar with Byzantium and may have little familiarity with

Byzantine Christianity. But no one who wishes to appreciate the Christian tradition both past and present in its fullness, or to understand past history and contemporary political developments, can afford to ignore either Byzantine Christianity or its legacy.

Glossary

apse   hemispherical space at the east end of a church, typically decorated in the Byzantine period with mosaics or frescoes

Asia Minor   western region of modern Turkey, sometimes also used of regions further east

autocephaly   in post-Byzantine period, independence granted to a regional Orthodox church by the ecumenical patriarch, together with permission to have a patriarch

basilica   typical example of early Byzantine church architecture, derived from Roman public buildings, with nave, apse (see above) and side aisles

Bogomils   religious sect mainly in the medieval Balkans, believing in two competing divine principles, good and evil

bull, papal   papal document (from *bulla*, referring to the papal seal)

Caesaropapism   older theory that the Byzantine emperor controlled the church, no longer held

catechetical   relating to catechesis, the instruction given to candidates for baptism

catholicos   head of the Armenian Church, equivalent to patriarch

cenobitic   type of monastic organization, based on the idea of a communal life

Cumans   Turkic people, threat to Byzantium in Comnenian period

Epirus   region in what is now north-west Greece and Albania, location of the Despotate of Epirus in the late Byzantine period

ethnophyletism negative term used in Orthodox circles for the conflation of nationalism and religion

exarchate limited level of local religious independence

hagiography term for the overall production of written lives of saints

homilies in Greek, equivalent of Latin term 'sermons', used in early Christian, Byzantine and Orthodox contexts

iconoclasm opposition to, and sometimes acts of destruction against, icons (also used loosely to denote the period of the iconoclastic controversy in Byzantium, from 726 or 730 to 843)

iconostasis screen in later Byzantine and Orthodox churches marking off the sanctuary and the altar, on which icons are displayed

Kievan Rus' conventionally, the period during which the Rus' were based at Kiev, from the late ninth century to the Mongol invasion of 1240

Latins term used by the Byzantines to denote western Christians (and Crusaders)

liturgy Byzantine and Orthodox religious service, also the term used for the Eucharist or Mass

metropolitan archbishop (Byzantine and Orthodox hierarch between the bishops and the patriarch)

minuscule Greek cursive script used from the ninth century, replacing previous style of writing entirely in capitals (majuscule, uncial)

'Nestorian' term often mistakenly used of the East Syrian Church of the East, after Nestorius

Ottomans Turkic ruling dynasty from thirteenth century onwards, conquerors of Constantinople, 1453; founders of the Ottoman empire, replaced in 1923 by Republic of Turkey

Pannonia   Roman province on the Danube, north of Italy, later used of the same area of central Europe

patriarch   one of the five patriarchs of the early Church (Rome, Antioch, Alexandria, Jerusalem, Constantinople); often refers in the Byzantine period to the patriarch of Constantinople; in modern Orthodoxy, used of the 'ecumenical patriarch' based in Istanbul, or the head of a church granted autocephaly (see above)

Paulicians   group with dualist beliefs similar to Bogomils (see above), based in Armenia and eastern Turkey, seventh to ninth centuries

Pechenegs   Turkic steppe people who migrated westwards and alternately allied with and fought the Byzantines; defeated in eleventh and twelfth centuries; served also as Byzantine mercenaries

Seljuks   Turkic dynasties ruling in Persia, Syria and Turkey, eleventh century to early fourteenth; inflicted major defeat on the Byzantines at Manzikert in eastern Turkey, AD 1071

syllogism   form of logical argument based on deductive reasoning and in three parts, defined by Aristotle; much used by both sides in Byzantine religious debate with the Latins

synod   ecclesiastical assembly, usually local (contrasted with councils; see Chapter 3); also of permanent 'standing synod' or ecclesiastical assembly in Constantinople

Syriac   the version of Aramaic originally used in Mesopotamia; became an important literary and theological language throughout the Byzantine period from the fourth century onwards

tetrarchs   four emperors who shared power in the Roman empire in system established by Diocletian, AD 293; ended when Constantine became sole emperor (also tetrarchy, tetrarchic)

Thrace   Roman and Byzantine district; term loosely used for the European hinterland of Constantinople; now split between Greece, Bulgaria and Turkey

Umayyads   Arab dynasty ruling in Syria from 661 to 750, with capital at Damascus

uncial   Greek script written in capitals (also 'majuscule', and replaced by minuscule – see above)

Further reading

General

Ken Parry, David J. Melling, Dimitri Brady, Sidney H. Griffith and John F. Healey (eds), *The Blackwell Dictionary of Eastern Christianity*, Oxford: Blackwell, 1999.

Ken Parry (ed.), *The Blackwell Companion to Eastern Christianity*, Oxford: Blackwell, 2007.

Two comprehensive reference works covering all aspects of eastern Christianity up to the present day.

1 What was Byzantium?

Judith Herrin, *Byzantium: The Surprising Life of a Medieval Empire*, London: Allen Lane, 2007.

Averil Cameron, *The Byzantines*, Oxford: Wiley-Blackwell, 2006.

Accessible recent introductions to Byzantium.

2 Monks, monasteries and bishops

Averil Cameron, *The Later Roman Empire, AD 284–430*, London: Fontana Press, 1993.

Peter Brown, *The World of Late Antiquity: From Marcus Aurelius to Muhammad*, London: Thames & Hudson, 1971.

Introductions to the period, covering Constantine's support for Christianity and religious change in the eastern empire.

3 The age of the Fathers

Peter Brown, *Power and Persuasion in Late Antiquity: Towards a Christian Empire*, Madison, IL: University of Wisconsin Press, 1992.

Peter Brown, *Authority and the Sacred: Aspects of the Christianisation of the Roman World*, Cambridge: Cambridge University Press, 1995.

Two short books about Christianization by a master historian.

4 The eastern Church splits

Derwas Chitty, *The Desert a City: An Introduction to the Study of Egyptian and Palestinian Monasticism under the Christian Empire*, London: Mowbray's, 1966.

The beginnings of Christian asceticism and monasticism in the east.

Averil Cameron, *The Mediterranean World in Late Antiquity, AD 395–700*, 2nd edn, London: Routledge, 2011.

Covers the crucial period that included the emergence of Islam.

5 Icons and iconoclasm

Mark Whittow, *The Making of Orthodox Byzantium, 600–1025*, London: Macmillan, 1996.

Covers the period of the 'dark ages' and the subsequent Byzantine recovery.

Robin Cormack, *Icons*, London: British Museum, 2014.

Icons explained by a leading art historian.

6 After iconoclasm

Andrew Louth, *Greek East and Latin West: The Church, AD 681–1071*, Crestwood, NY: St. Vladimir's Seminary Press, 2007.

Traces the connections and tensions between eastern and western Christianity up to and including 1054.

Dimitri Obolensky, *The Byzantine Commonwealth: Eastern Europe, 500–1453*, London: Weidenfeld & Nicolson, 1971.

Classic book on Byzantine relations with other states and peoples in eastern Europe.

Graham Speake, *Mount Athos: Renewal in Paradise*, New Haven, CT and London: Yale University Press, 2002.

Mount Athos and its monasteries.

7 The Macedonian emperors

Stephenson, Paul, *The Legend of Basil the Bulgar-Slayer*, Cambridge: Cambridge University Press, 2003.
The intriguing story of how the Emperor Basil II became a legend.
Henry Chadwick, *East and West: The Making of a Rift in the Church. From Apostolic Times until the Council of Florence*, Oxford: Oxford University Press, 2003.
History of east–west church relations throughout the Byzantine period.

8 Byzantium under the Comneni

Anna Komnene, *The Alexiad*, trans. E. R. A. Sewter, revised with introduction and notes by Peter Frankopan, London: Penguin, 2009.
Fascinating history of her father's reign by a woman historian.
Peter Frankopan, *The First Crusade: The Call from the East*, London: Bodley Head, 2012.
A view of the First Crusade with emphasis on the Byzantine perspective.
Averil Cameron, *Arguing it Out: Discussion in Twelfth-Century Byzantium*, Princeton, NJ: Princeton University Press, 2016.
Religious debates in Comnenian Byzantium.

9 1204 and after

Jonathan Harris, Catherine Holmes and Eugenia Russell (eds), *Byzantines, Latins, and Turks in the Eastern Mediterranean World after 1150*, Oxford: Oxford University Press, 2012.
On the complex relationships and changed situation in the eastern Mediterranean from the late twelfth century onwards.
Michael Angold, *A Byzantine Government in Exile: Government and Society under the Laskarids of Nicaea, 1204–1261*, Oxford: Oxford University Press, 1975.
A study of Byzantine rule at Nicaea.

Clive Foss, with Jacob Tulchin, *Nicaea: A Byzantine Capital and its Praises, with the Speeches of Theodore Laskaris, In Praise of the Great City of Nicaea, and Theodore Metochites, Nicene Oration*, Brookline, MA: Hellenic College Press, 1996.

A window into the cultural and intellectual life maintained by the court in exile at Nicaea from 1204 to 1261.

10 Byzantium 1261–1453

Steven Runciman, *The Fall of Constantinople, 1453*, Cambridge: Cambridge University Press, 2012 (first published 1965).

Classic telling of the tragic events in 1453.

Donald Nicol, *The Immortal Emperor: The Life and Legend of Constantine Palaiologos, Last Emperor of Byzantium*, Cambridge: Cambridge University Press, 1992.

The strange story of Constantine XI and his legend.

11 Byzantium and Orthodox life and spirituality

Derek Krueger (ed.), *Byzantine Christianity*, A People's History of Christianity 3, Minneapolis, MN: Fortress Press, 2006.

Lay experience of Christian worship in Byzantium.

Mary B. Cunningham, *Faith in the Byzantine World*, Oxford: Lion Publishing, 2002.

A brief sympathetic survey of Christian life in Byzantium.

Cyril Mango, *Byzantium: The Empire of New Rome*, London: Weidenfeld & Nicolson, 1980.

An astringent look at Byzantium and its religion from a very different point of view.

12 The setting of worship

Robin Cormack, *Byzantine Art*, Oxford: Oxford University Press, 2000.

Excellent general guide to Byzantine art.

Cyril Mango, *Byzantine Architecture*, London: Faber/Electa, 1986 (first published New York: Rizzoli, 1978).

Beautifully illustrated general coverage of the history and development of architecture in the Byzantine world.

13 Discipline and control

Michael Angold, *Church and Society in Byzantium under the Comneni, 1081–1261*, Cambridge: Cambridge University Press, 1995.

Joan M. Hussey, *The Orthodox Church in the Byzantine Empire*, Oxford: Clarendon Press, 1986.

Both standard academic guides.

14 Orthodox churches and others

Steven Runciman, *The Great Church in Captivity*, Cambridge: Cambridge University Press, 1968.

Classic work on the Orthodox Church under Ottoman rule.

Dimitri Obolensky, *Byzantium and the Slavs*, Crestwood, NY: St. Vladimir's Seminary Press, 1994.

The influence of Byzantine Christianity on the Slavonic world.

John A. McGuckin, *The Orthodox Church: An Introduction to its History, Doctrine and Spiritual Culture*, Oxford: Blackwell, 2008.

Especially useful on the national and diaspora varieties of Orthodoxy and their history.

15 Perspectives today

John A. McGuckin, *Standing in God's Holy Fire: The Byzantine Tradition*, London: Darton, Longman & Todd, 2001.

Augustine Casiday (ed.), *The Orthodox Christian World*, Abingdon: Routledge, 2012.

On the Orthodox world including the Byzantine tradition.

Index

Index

Index

Index

Index

Index

Index

Index

Printed and bound by CPI Group (UK) Ltd, Croydon, CR0 4YY

16/09/2024

14557805-0001